THE Happiness CRISIS

THE Happiness CRISIS

HOW ADVERSITY CAN BUILD A RESILIENT AND JOYFUL NEXT GENERATION

JONATHAN ECKERT

W Publishing Group
An Imprint of Thomas Nelson

The Happiness Crisis

Published by W Publishing, an imprint of Thomas Nelson, 501 Nelson Place, Nashville, TN 37214, USA.

Published in association with Don Gates—The Gates Group, www.the-gates-group.com.

Thomas Nelson titles may be purchased in bulk for educational, business, fundraising, or sales promotional use. For information, please email SpecialMarkets@ThomasNelson.com.

ISBN 978-1-4003-5654-6 (audiobook)
ISBN 978-1-4003-5653-9 (ePub)
ISBN 978-1-4003-5650-8 (TP)

HarperCollins Publishers, Macken House, 39/40 Mayor Street Upper, Dublin 1, D01 C9W8, Ireland (https://www.harpercollins.com)

Library of Congress Control Number: 2026935429

Printed in the United States of America

26 27 28 29 30 LBC 5 4 3 2 1

For Carolyn—thanks for your wisdom and our joy.

CONTENTS

PART 1: KIDS ARE HEADING THE WRONG WAY FOR WELL-LIVED LIVES

Chapter 1: Trying to Be Happy Is Making Kids Miserable 3
Chapter 2: None of Us Saw the Dead-End Road Sign 18
Chapter 3: Back to the ABCs 31
Chapter 4: The Path to the Good Life 44

PART 2: LIFE IS HARD *AND* JOYFUL

Chapter 5: Kids Grow Up by Doing Hard Things 63
Chapter 6: TikTok Is Not Truth 81
Chapter 7: Echo Chambers Breed Insecurity 98
Chapter 8: Help Kids Own Their Stories 112
Chapter 9: Stop Pushing Self-Care Culture on Kids 122

PART 3: A HOSPITABLE WELCOME TO A BETTER WAY

Chapter 10: Our Job Is Not to Make Kids Comfortable 139
Chapter 11: Kids Seek Status, Not Safetyism 155
Chapter 12: Hospitality Means Kids Matter 172
Chapter 13: Chase Progress, Not Success 183

Acknowledgments 203
Notes 205
About the Author 231

PART 1

KIDS ARE HEADING THE WRONG WAY FOR WELL-LIVED LIVES

"We just want our kids to be happy."

I hear this from parents all over the world. But how are the kids doing? If this is what parents want, why aren't kids happier?

I refer to kids as anyone who is not yet an adult.[1] Over three decades, I have taught young people from ages nine to twenty-two. At their core, they have not changed. They still want to belong and to matter. We adults, however, have sent them down a path in pursuit of happiness that is a dead end. Their ears are plugged with noise-canceling headphones, their necks are bent in ways that build a client base for chiropractors, and no one is talking. Embodied souls sit side by side in the real world, unaware it has become distorted by a mesmerizing virtual world.

Take a walk through a park, down a street, or around a college campus—you'll see that students are proximate but alone. In pursuit of virtual happiness, they miss joy in the physical world that can be found with the people around them.[2]

This is not another book about the evils of social media, the addictiveness of smartphones, or an anxious generation. This book explores what those of us who work with kids encounter as a result of the epidemic that is "happiness culture." Success is economic and expected. Happiness is immediate and life's ultimate prize.

In a mad pursuit of ephemeral happiness, we are training our kids to believe that if they are struggling, they are not well.

To change course, we need to first identify what is wrong with that path kids are currently on . . .

1
TRYING TO BE HAPPY IS MAKING KIDS MISERABLE

Years ago, when I was a middle-school science teacher and basketball coach, I spent many hours with a student named Dante.[1] He was always doing one of two things: smiling or talking. I often wanted him to talk less to his friends while we were moving through a dissection or drill, but I always appreciated his buoyancy, whether he failed a science lab or was relegated to the end of the basketball bench. He left for high school on a promising path surrounded by many friends.

I never would have guessed that one day, messages from former students would flood my phone reporting a tragedy: As a senior in high school, Dante died by suicide. From what I was able to gather from his friends and social media, although he appeared to have a well-curated virtual presence, he'd felt increasingly isolated and depressed throughout his high-school years. The online persona of a flourishing kid with a lot of friends was only a facade for a lonely, hurting human being.

Dante's story is tragically common, as more than 20 percent of high-school students have seriously considered suicide, 16 percent report making a suicide plan in the past year,[2] and 10 percent have attempted suicide.[3] This reality appears to be related to the isolation, depression, and anxiety that has coincided with ubiquitous smartphones, social media, and front-facing cameras since 2010.

- Reported anxiety in eighteen-to-twenty-five-year-olds increased by *161 percent*.[4]
- Reported major depressive episodes for U.S. teens increased by *133 percent* for girls and *188 percent* for boys.[5]
- U.S. emergency department visits for self-harm (ages ten to fourteen) increased by *286 percent* for girls and *143 percent* for boys.[6]
- The U.S. teen suicide rate (ages fifteen to nineteen) increased by *58 percent* for girls and *27 percent* for boys.[7]
- In the most recently reported year, we lost *6,533* ten-to-twenty-four-year-olds to suicide.[8]

The fight for the next generation is a life-or-death struggle.

We lose that generation one individual at a time. Suicide is the tragic end to a path that begins with rejection, depression, anxiety, and isolation, for which there are many causes. Over the past few years, much has been written about the role of technology, substances, and polarized culture that seem to be eroding community. Whatever the cause, kids are dying to be happy. Those of us pouring into the next generation can confirm the reality is bleak.

THE NUMBERS DON'T LIE

The next several paragraphs are a statistical tsunami of disheartening data. As you read, please keep the real faces of kids in mind. Kids like Dante. Kids like the young people in your life. This book will be driven by their narratives. These narratives are descriptions of human experiences that we must not look away from. Our job is to not let the numbers hide the faces that make them up.

Many kids are anxious, depressed, and tired.[9] Of U.S. kids ages three to seventeen, one in five have been diagnosed with a mental, emotional, or behavioral health condition, and one in ten have a diagnosed anxiety disorder.[10] Of twelve-to-seventeen-year-olds, 16 percent have an anxiety-disorder diagnosis, which is up 61 percent since 2016. Another 8 percent have a depression-disorder diagnosis, which is up 45 percent since 2016.[11] We know kids with anxiety disorders are less likely to perform well in school and more likely to engage in substance abuse.[12] Nearly four in ten U.S. high-school students report persistent feelings of sadness and hopelessness.[13] Whether part cause or effect, over half of teenage girls and nearly half of teenage boys report getting less than seven hours of sleep a night,[14] and 36 percent wake up at least once a night to check a device because nearly 70 percent of them take their devices to bed.[15] Another study found that 78 percent of eleven-to-thirteen-year-olds own a smartphone. Of those kids, one in four sleeps with it in their hands.[16] Based on data from more than 10,500 children, kids who had a smartphone by the age of twelve were at higher risk of depression, obesity, and insufficient sleep than those who did not have one.[17]

More kids are isolated and lonely. Since 2010, for fifteen-to-twenty-four-year-olds, daily time with friends in the real world has dropped from over two hours to forty-three minutes—a 67 percent decrease.[18] Over 40 percent of boys do not have friends that they can "get together with," and the same is true of about 35 percent of girls. Nearly 50 percent of teenage girls and nearly 30 percent of boys report often feeling lonely.[19]

Kids are trying to find community online. For boys in the United States between the ages of eleven and seventeen, 94 percent are online daily. More than half, 62 percent, play video games with chat features each day. Over half, 58 percent, say they find a sense of belonging in gaming, but 70 percent say they have witnessed bullying or harassing as well.[20]

I am not convinced spending more time online is the cure to loneliness—but we do need a cure. Loneliness and social isolation carry health risks similar to smoking fifteen cigarettes per day and can increase the risk of premature death by more than 26 percent.[21]

Kids lack purpose. Since 2010, we have seen a 100 percent increase in the number of teenage boys who do not see their lives as useful and a 155 percent increase for teenage girls. For those same kids, there has been a 138 percent increase for girls and a 75 percent increase for boys who feel that life is meaningless.[22]

Are the depressing numbers above the fault of smartphones, social media, political polarization, the breakdown of the family, poor education, bad therapy, overmedication of kids, or ineffective parenting? We can find books that would support or refute any of these claims.[23] Quantitative social scientists always want to quantify a problem and find the cause, which is a worthy pursuit. In their attempt to quantify and find a root cause, however, they can oversimplify complex issues that have many causes.

I will pause here to make the disclaimer that I am not a psychologist, sociologist, historian, neurologist, cognitive scientist, philosopher, or theologian. I am a parent, professor, and coach who, like many of you, is trying to make sense of an increasingly complex world and build a path to greater joy for young people. While citing evidence from many fields, I am interpreting it through the lens of my thirty years as an educator and twenty-three years as a parent.[24]

Regardless of the reasons behind our current reality, parenting, education, and coaching remain three of our greatest levers to change narratives. Rather than getting stuck debating the exact causes of these numbers, we need to understand the overarching narrative of what we experience with kids each day. Narratives are not just entertaining stories; they are people, events, and places woven together in ways that shape and influence reality.[25]

The numbers above mirror our lived reality, don't they? The most common descriptions teens give of their experience in school are "stressed, tired, and bored."[26] Walk into many schools and you will see kids who are passively disengaged. On a recent high-school visit, every classroom I sat in had at least one kid who was asleep. High-school bathrooms without vape detectors contain kids (at least 1.63 million kids in the United States)[27] inhaling fumes from vapes, filling their lungs with who-knows-what to deal with stress, boredom, or anxiety.

I direct the Baylor Center for School Leadership, and for the past three years, we have been working with middle and high schools in rural Mississippi at the epicenter of the opioid epidemic. Educators tell us, "We try to show kids how life is better without substances, but they go home to trailers with parents who are passed out on couches." Kids are searching for meaning in a broken world, where the adults around them are sometimes lost.

Sometimes the adults are not lost, but they still send kids down the path to substance dependence out of a desire to help. Danielle was a seven-year-old at a private girls' school in Philadelphia. On the recommendation of the school, her mom took her to a psychiatrist to get an attention-deficit/hyperactivity disorder (ADHD) diagnosis and was prescribed a stimulant. The stimulant made Danielle "agitated, moody and angry," so another doctor added Prozac to her medication. Twenty-two years later, Danielle had taken fourteen different psychiatric drugs.

While different from the opioid crisis, both approaches lead to misery through the overuse of substances and miss what will lead to a meaningful life.[28]

Is it possible that kids are on the wrong path because we have pointed them in the wrong direction?

HOLLOW HAPPINESS

Ask a teenager what makes them happy. If you can get past the shrug and the "I don't know" as their eyes return to a screen, what kind of answers might you get?

"You, leaving me alone."

"Playing video games with my friends."

"My phone."

My sense is that many kids think happiness is found online, where they feel safe behind a screen—less vulnerable than in a real world that is becoming increasingly scary to them. They prefer snaps or texts to speaking on the phone, and view calling someone without texting first as aggressive. Kids are sacrificing sleep to stay connected online. On average, sixteen-to-seventeen-year-olds are on their phones for at least a few minutes every hour of the day.[29] Almost 30 percent of teenagers report sleeping with their phones in their beds to get notifications.[30] How can they feel happy when their sleep is constantly interrupted by a virtual world that is trying to sell their attention as a product?

Gen Z is on pace to spend more than twenty-five years of their lives on smartphones.[31] Yet they're finding themselves feeling increasingly isolated and unhappy. It's apparent the virtual happiness they are pursuing is hollow and exhausting.

Regardless of how we define *happiness*, at some level, kids have to be satisfied with themselves. Since 2010 we have seen an alarming drop in the percentage of kids who are satisfied with themselves. One in two twelfth-grade girls and one in three twelfth-grade boys is not satisfied with themselves. In 2010, 78 percent of boys were satisfied with themselves and ten years later that number dropped to 64 percent. For girls, the drop was even greater from 74 percent to 54 percent.[32] What happens when they don't feel like they measure up to the expectations of parents, teachers, or coaches? If they believe that we will only be content with them if they achieve a level of success, contentment will likely be elusive.

Much of this seems to correlate with a lack of purpose, something that many experts have found matters a great deal for life satisfaction and joy.[33]

In *Man's Search for Meaning,* Viktor Frankl described his journey to a life of meaning after surviving Nazi concentration camps. He determined that "the meaning of your life is to help others find the meaning in theirs." Frankl developed logotherapy, a form of psychotherapy focused on helping individuals find meaning and purpose in their lives, even amid suffering.

Looks like our kids might need logotherapy. Maybe that is the answer—"Find your own meaning"?

Or, conversely, maybe the answer is finding meaning in parents' purpose for their kids. As parents, we know best, right? Take these three statements I hear from parents:

PARENT #1 TO KID: "If you would just put some effort into [sport, instrument, or vocational pursuit], I know you could be great."

PARENT #2 TO KID: "I love that you are reading books. You are so smart. That is what smart adults do."

PARENT #3 TO KID: "You can be anything you want to be. Just follow your passion."

Whether they acknowledge it or not, kids desire affirmation from their parents. I might have said all the statements above to my own kids at some point, and they all have some hint of truth. The problem is, they communicate that happiness is tied to performance and hypothesize a path to happiness.

When parents say these kinds of things, here is what they are communicating at least in part about happiness:

PARENT #1 TO KID: "If you work really hard and become great, you will have my approval and be successful, which will lead to happiness."

The problematic message here is that a human's value is based solely on performance.

PARENT #2 TO KID: "Intelligence is a fixed trait and is valuable. You will be happy if you are smart."

The problem here is that it is better to view intelligence as something that can be developed, not as a fixed trait.[34]

In fact, University of Virginia cognitive scientist Dan Willingham has found that "it is never smart to tell a child she's smart. Believe it or not, doing so makes her less smart."[35] He is a father of a severely mentally disabled child. "My daughter is not intelligent in any sense of the word," Willingham wrote. But he also described her as "a joyful child who brings a lot of happiness to a lot of people."[36]

That is hard to read, right? I know it is for me because I subconsciously equate intelligence with value.

PARENT #3 TO KID: "Passion leads to happiness, and you can find happiness in anything you choose."

Two problems here: Passions are not always the initial motivation for perseverance, and kids cannot be anything they want to be.

As kids develop skills and gain recognition for those skills, sometimes passions follow. Consider: How many three-year-olds are truly passionate about learning the violin?

Second, telling kids they can be whatever they want to be is just not true. No matter how much I dream, at six feet, four inches tall, I will never be a jockey.[37] Kids have been given skills and talents that they can cultivate to the point of value. They do not have every skill or talent. Telling them they do can be paralyzing.[38]

Not surprisingly, many kids are not finding happiness on these paths. Increasingly, young-adult self-help books are telling them not to worry about what others think about them and to find their own meaning.[39] Two of the most popular titles on the market are *The Courage to Be Disliked* (more than ten million copies sold) and *The Subtle Art of Not Giving a F*ck* (more than sixteen million copies sold).

Maybe that is the answer? Kids just need to focus more on themselves, their truth, and what makes them happy—and forget about everyone else?

This seems to be the mindset of adults and the way many of us approach our own lives.

THE EPIDEMIC OF "HAPPINESS CULTURE"

Happiness is something we all chase. Thomas Jefferson wrote the "pursuit of happiness" into the Declaration of Independence.[40] The concept is everywhere, from advertisements to fairy tales that end in "happily ever after." We live in a world filled with people who believe that they should pursue their own happiness—and that pursuit is making them miserable.

Part of the problem is the mixed messages of what happiness is. A search of the word *happy* on Amazon Books produces over seventy thousand results with at least as many definitions of that word.

An article with the headline "24 Must-Read Happiness Books"

lists titles like *Shine*, *The Happy High Achiever*, *MicroSkills*, *Think like Socrates*, and *The New Happy*. Just reading these titles makes me exhausted.

Is happiness something that must be achieved?

Every year since 2012, the United Nations has conducted a survey and released the World Happiness Report that ranks countries by happiness. The report is based on one question: "Please imagine a ladder with steps numbered from 0 at the bottom to 10 at the top. The top of the ladder represents the best possible life for you and the bottom of the ladder represents the worst possible life for you. On which step of the ladder would you say you personally feel you stand at this time?"[41]

Is happiness just living your best life based on your perception of how you measure the rungs on your imaginary ladder?

You can take a *New York Times* online quiz to determine if you are happy.[42] The quiz asks sixteen questions about what you have experienced in the past year, including: Have you "eaten or drunk something uniquely, unforgettably delicious?" "Worked on a new skill or hobby?" "Enjoyed dancing to a favorite song?"

When you finish, your happiness score is a pie chart that tells you whether you have good balance between hedonic well-being (short-term pleasure and avoiding pain) and eudaemonic well-being (the sense of purpose and connection to others). If you are balanced, then you are more likely to be happy.

Is happiness simply equivalent to well-being?

Happiness is such a mystery that Harvard and Yale offer popular courses on it. Positive psychology asserts that we have a genetic predisposition toward either happiness or unhappiness, we are affected by external conditions, and we have some control over our actions that can increase or decrease our happiness. The father of positive psychology, Martin Seligman, has taught that if we cultivate kindness, originality, humor, optimism, and generosity, we can achieve authentic contentment, gratification, and meaning.[43]

Does happiness boil down to positive thinking?

Jonathan Haidt, a social psychologist and professor at New York University, argued in *The Happiness Hypothesis* that balancing the left brain and right brain is key. Just like a person riding a willful elephant cannot easily guide it by force, the rational mind cannot reason with strong emotions—so our feelings often end up controlling us. Once we learn to train our "elephant," such as through meditation, and influence it in a nurturing environment, we will be happier, Haidt contended.[44]

Gretchen Rubin, a lawyer by training, sold millions of copies of her book *The Happiness Project*, about her year of trying to be happier.[45] She offered many helpful tips and tricks to having more fun and finding happiness in closet cleaning and singing.

Arthur Brooks, Harvard professor, bestselling author, and social scientist, asserted that the key to happiness is managing your life in a way that leads to love, enjoyment, satisfaction, and meaning in *The Happiness Files*.[46] The book is a compilation of his *Atlantic* column, "How to Build a Good Life."

These authors represent a few of the many smart, thoughtful people who have given us a range of options that might get us to happiness—from genetics to tips, to training our elephant, to finding purpose, to managing our lives.

But are our kids even thinking about happiness this way?

Their brains are increasingly wired for instant gratification and self-focus. A hit of dopamine from a reel or a heart emoji in response to a curated picture of themselves feeds their happiness addiction—momentarily. Then they go back to feeling isolated, sad, and lonely, nowhere near the happiness described above.

Dante's face is seared into my brain when I read these descriptions of happiness. The kid I knew was charismatic, charming, and great at connecting with people. The kid he became behind his social-media persona was a stranger to me. From what I gathered from his friends, in his pursuit of happiness, he withered. Based on the evidence, we know he is not alone.

HAPPY CONFUSION

There is another approach to pursuing happiness we haven't discussed yet, one that educators have increasingly turned to the last several decades: mindfulness. Originating from Hinduism and Buddhism, many have found it helpful for focus and emotional regulation.[47] Certainly, this can be beneficial for actively noticing new things[48] and regulating stress,[49] but does increased self-focus typically lead to authentic happiness?

Let's see. Take a moment right now and focus on how you feel.

What is your emotional state?

What is your level of stress?

Do you feel anxiety?

How do you feel physically?

I spent decades playing basketball, which means that, at any given time, something hurts. I also am usually feeling some level of anxiety about work, family, or other stressors. On a happiness scale of zero to ten, with zero being an "emotional/physical puddle" and ten being "my best life," I am usually a seven.

How would you rate yourself?

No human can authentically live at the top of the scale all the time. If, at any point, we want to move up the scale, can we do so by focusing more on ourselves and how we feel on a regular basis?

That's not been my experience.

If we struggle to do this as adults, how are kids going to be able to get to happiness by focusing on their internal world? Are we just helping them be aware of their inner friends from Pixar's wildly popular movies *Inside Out* and *Inside Out 2*?

Parent/Educator: "Kids, focus on how you are feeling. Be aware of Joy, Sadness, Anger, Fear, and Disgust (your feelings from the first movie), then you can meet and regulate your new feelings from the second movie (Anxiety, Envy, Embarrassment, and Ennui) as you develop."

This is the kind of approach used in social-emotional learning songs for kids (a quick online search will yield no shortage of results). Kids learn to regulate by naming emotions, using a range of upbeat (if somewhat cringy) songs or dances, sitting quietly, and "tummy breathing." Focusing on the self, on the circumstances and feelings of the moment, brings clarity and calm.

Is mindfulness the key to happiness?

I can't help but wonder about the deeper need kids have to find their identity in something more stable, with a stronger foundation in a community that tells them that they matter.

When we compile all the most prominent research about finding happiness—from achieving it through self-improvement to emphasizing positive thinking or mindfulness—we end up with more questions than clear answers.

Here's another question for the list: How does happiness relate to well-being, flourishing, joy, and struggle? How do we define those things?

Here is a quick review of definitions:

- *happiness*: feeling or showing pleasure or contentment
- *well-being*: the state of being happy, healthy, or prosperous

- *flourishing*: developing rapidly and successfully
- *joy*: the state of happiness or felicity

Perhaps you noticed these four terms have overlapping meanings. Where does struggle fit? Where does "growth through discomfort" come in?

Young people want to be happy. It is possible that trying to be happy is making them miserable because they do not even know what it means to be happy. The definitions above can easily blur together and cause us to think young people simply need to pursue pleasure and good feelings and somehow curate a life with little to no adversity.

If we have led kids to believe that struggling isn't normal—something to be expected in life—we have sent them down a dead-end path. Do we honestly believe "just being happy" now as kids will form them into strong, capable adults who can weather the ups and downs of a lifetime?

In our moments of clarity, surely not.

So what can we do to help them?

That's what the rest of this book will answer.

Young people can experience something better than circumstantial happiness, a series of dopamine hits, a virtual escape, or easy wins. Instead, they need adults to support them in embracing challenges that shape them into stronger versions of themselves, so they can lead more joyful lives.

In the first part of this book, we'll continue exploring the kind of thinking that got us where we are with our kids and identify the role of struggle in the experience of joy. In the second and third parts, I will share stories and evidence from around the world of people experiencing joy through struggle with practical suggestions you can try with the young people in your life.

Drawing from evidence and my own experience as a parent, educator, and coach, I see a clear path forward for us. Yes, kids are not thriving, but they can. We adults can help them become a generation liberated by joy. We can cultivate the conditions for experiencing joy amid adversity by living with purpose, establishing a strong identity, and forming habits for long-term flourishing.

In the next chapter, we'll be taking a closer look at the role we've all played in putting kids on the path they're on today. While a good, fulfilling life is within their reach, they won't find it by following their instinct to chase what is easy.

TAKEAWAY

Pursuing happiness (in the way kids currently conceive of it) is leading to anxiety, depression, suicide, loneliness, and lack of purpose. What if joy is better? And what if joy is not something we pursue and instead is something that emerges?

TRY THIS

Ask a kid three questions:

1. How do you define *happiness*?
2. What do you do to try to get more of it?
3. How is that working for you?

2

NONE OF US SAW THE DEAD-END ROAD SIGN

Do you know what a "lawn-mower parent" or a "lawn-mower educator" is?

It is an adult who goes beyond merely hovering over a kid like a helicopter, as the previous generation did. Out of a desire to help young people be happy, lawn-mower adults actually remove any obstacle that might cause kids to struggle.

Here are examples of how this can look with different age groups.

Elementary lawn-mower parent example: "My child cannot be in that first-grade classroom because those three boys were mean to him last year in kindergarten. I am the head room mom for first grade, and I know that teacher cannot handle those boys." The move was made, and the mom was in the more-desirable classroom, looking out for her kid on a weekly basis to ensure fair play at recess and adequate opportunities for connecting with the "right families" at the school.

Middle-school lawn-mower educator example: In discussing rampant cheating, a parent raised a concern to a middle-school principal.

He responded without blinking an eye, "Well, at least they are learning how to collaborate." Turning a blind eye to students claiming work that is not their own, let alone their best work, and just ensuring that something is turned in is "lawn-mower education."

High-school lawn-mower parent example: During the COVID-19 pandemic school shutdown, a parent posted her son's precalculus exam on Facebook to crowdsource answers. When her son got a C on the exam, she protested to the teacher that it was not a very good test "because we had a mathematician review the test and his answers were different."

College lawn-mower parent example: A parent of a college freshman reaching out to a college professor says, "We got our daughter an ADHD diagnosis last year, so she can have extended time on her exams. She needs a separate space to take the exam and should be able to use her notes from class because she cannot be expected to remember auditory classroom input due to her disability."

Parents mean well. We want our kids to be successful. What we do not realize is that all four of these examples rob kids of the chance to actually achieve success. We can unknowingly lead them to feel incompetent and develop learned helplessness. Researchers have recently found that when adults intervene too early with kids who are struggling with something, the kids report feeling less capable.[1] A recent research article examining forty-four studies found that overparenting actually increased kids' depression and anxiety.[2]

The elementary parent robs the kid of the chance to work through adversity with others with relatively low six-year-old-kid stakes. The middle-school principal misses the opportunity to give kids honest feedback on how to grow because he does not know what students are capable of doing on their own. The high-school parent denies the kid the opportunity to learn by off-loading learning to crowdsourcing.

The college parent has gotten a diagnosis (perhaps without even a real need)[3] and is using the disability to prop up success without learning—while also not allowing the college student to advocate for her own needs, a skill in and of itself.[4]

Even getting into college is something lawn-mower parents are now managing. A colleague who works in admissions at a large state university expressed frustration to me that parents were completing over 30 percent of the applications for admission.

"How do you know they're doing it?" I asked.

"When we call the phone number listed on the application, it is a parent's number, and they want to ask questions about the application," he replied.

College administrators have a new term for lawn-mower parents who persist into college: the "trailing parent," according to a recent article in *The Atlantic*. Parents are renting apartments or buying condos to facilitate frequent visits, some even trailing their kids on study-abroad trips, "moving for a semester to Florence or Barcelona to be close 'just in case.'" Helicopter parents used to attempt to manage college students' lives from a distance, but "the trailing parent touches down." At George Washington University, they had to tell a mom that "she wasn't actually permitted to sit next to her kid in class."[5] Sounds to me like the lawn-mower parent is coming to a college near you.

This type of parenting is not resulting in better outcomes for young people. A report from the University of California at San Diego, the sixth-best public university in the United States,[6] found that 8 percent of its entering class for 2025 needed a class to remediate elementary- and middle-school math.[7] Maybe they just need Mom sitting next to them in the elementary math class at college.

Teachers mean well. The average anxious student receives twenty school-based supports. Most are avoidance-based supports that provide extra time for tests, separate spaces in which to work, and reduced workload.[8] Imagine an anxious kid who does not want to speak in front of a class having to give an oral report in eleventh-grade English class. He gets a note from a psychologist that recommends excusing him from the assignment and the school administration agrees. Two psychologists, one at Columbia University and the other at Harvard Medical School, describe the problems with this approach:

> Academic accommodations for anxiety convey two harmful messages. First, they imply that the feared situation is truly dangerous. Public speaking, testing, or lunch with classmates are too risky for a student. Second, they suggest that the student can't withstand the distress. Those messages increase anxiety.
>
> By contrast, when students take on what they'd rather avoid, they learn that worst-case scenarios rarely materialize, that discomfort is survivable, and that anxiety diminishes with practice. Indeed, purposely facing fears is the core of exposure therapy, the gold standard treatment for anxiety disorders for over half a century.[9]

Once we start down this path of removing barriers, it is hard to stop.

Many students are also succumbing to the allure of increasingly prevalent shortcuts. Professors are receiving doctoral dissertations in which they detect over 80 percent AI composition. This paper is the final step in a terminal degree, the highest level of study in a field, and a doctoral student's primary contribution, and it is being off-loaded to AI. If we do not want kids to miss out on true development and success by taking shortcuts, we have to call them to something better, so they become people who pursue excellence with integrity.

All over the world, I hear from parents:

"Our kids are not growing up."

"I cannot get my kid to do anything."

"You want my kid to serve someone else? I cannot even get him to clean up his room!"

"What is wrong with kids today?"

Kids are still kids. If there is something wrong with kids today, we as adults are largely to blame, even if we did not intend to send them down a dead-end path that leads to a stunted adulthood. If kids can get away without cleaning up a room and not serving others while being served by us, I can almost guarantee that any kid at any point in history would have taken full advantage. The crowdsourced precalculus test would have been the stuff of dreams for kids in the 1950s. Teachers turning a blind eye to cheating would have made it much more enticing as well. Getting to be in class without any of the kids I did not like would have been a dream for me. And don't even get me started on the chance to use my notes on an exam—summa cum laude, here I come!

When we do not give our kids the opportunity to struggle, we rob them of the chance to experience real and lasting success. Kids may think they have been successful because they have been gently parented and had all obstacles removed, but simply racking up a wall of participation trophies will not lead them to become fully developed adults, much less successful, happy adults. One day they will see through the facade, and far from being happy, they will be pretty frustrated.

EXPECTATIONS AND HAPPINESS

In many ways, there has never been a tougher time to be a parent or educator because things can be so easy and entitlement is so rampant.

This is particularly problematic for happiness because happiness is circumstantial.

The 1950s had many challenges, but as a decade, sociologists report that Americans were happy with their circumstances. The average household had a car, a home, a median household income of $29,000 (adjusted for inflation) a year, with groceries taking about 29 percent of that budget.[10] Today, the average family owns two cars, a home that is 172 percent larger,[11] and has a median household income of $80,610,[12] with groceries taking about 5 percent of that budget.[13] Yet people are significantly less happy than they were in the 1950s about their life situation.[14] Why?

Happiness is dependent on expectations. In the 1950s, families were emerging from the Great Depression and a war against the Nazis. These bleak realities shifted people's expectations and set a lower bar for happiness.

When reality exceeds expectations, we are happy. When reality does not meet expectations, we are disappointed. As our expectations rise, as they have since the 1950s, reality has less of a chance to exceed our expectations, reducing the likelihood that we will be happy.

We live in a time when things can be easy and entitlement is rampant. We expect success *and* the ability to avoid struggle at all costs. And as parents, we want our kids to make us look good. To that end, we say we want our kids to be challenged—but do we really?

Think of expectations here working on two levels: what we expect of our lives as parents, and what we expect of our kids. Many parents today expect their kids to make travel volleyball teams, get all A's, win state-level music competitions, maintain robust lists of extracurriculars, sustain "appropriate" levels of popularity, start nonprofits to end hunger, become parliamentarian of the National

Honor Society, campaign for class president, and gain entrance into prestigious colleges—all with the least amount of resistance for both the kids and parents.

Take Harvard-Westlake as an example. Harvard-Westlake is one of the most elite private schools in Los Angeles, California, with a tuition of $50,000 per year, and 17 percent of its 2024 graduates going to Ivy League schools. More is expected of the students. More is expected of the school. In recent years, Harvard-Westlake hired a director of wellness, relaxed grading policies, paired students with counselors, brought in comfort puppies, and used sidewalk chalk for positive messages. Even with these interventions and more resources than most schools could imagine, over a two-year period, four students, two alumni, and one parent have taken their own lives.[15]

For many parents, mental health means freedom from struggle (for both kids and parents). If families view struggle as something that impedes happiness and harms well-being, then we have a huge problem.

For other families, pressure to achieve drives kids to the point where they feel they can never do enough and do not see a way out. The obsession with status markers breeds trauma and hopelessness.

Whether we constantly try to remove obstacles from our kids' lives or pile on Herculean expectations—or do both—we've sent a message to kids about what happiness is and how they should pursue it.

The trouble is that directly pursuing happiness isn't going to get kids far.

British economist John Kay wrote, "Through experiences we normally associate with unhappiness, [people] achieve greater happiness than if they had sought happiness directly."[16]

If Kay is right that we do not typically experience happiness through direct pursuit, then what does that mean for us?

Think about yourself for a moment. What have you done to pursue happiness this week? What about today?

How is that working?

Maybe, like many adults, you have settled for scrolling on TikTok, Instagram, or YouTube as some form of connection or entertainment. It's likely become more of a default behavior, not an intentional path toward an overall happy life.

If we go back to the happiness quiz from chapter 1, maybe we think we get to happiness by picking up a hobby, reading a good book, or eating a delicious meal. If you've prioritized something like that, it might have given you a boost this week or today, but how do these momentary highlights stack up over a lifetime? While they are good, worthwhile experiences, when you put them together, do they become a formula for happiness?

John Kay would say no.

If happiness cannot be pursued directly, then why do we keep saying we just want our kids to be happy? Is that a destination we have to get to circuitously? Or is happiness even a destination we can reach?

I am asking all of these questions, but I do not have all the answers, which makes it all the more difficult to have these answers for kids. Even so, I believe we all have an inkling that there is something more to meaningful living.

I think struggle is a key.

THE OVERLOOKED VALUE OF STRUGGLE

In two of his books, Jonathan Haidt has highlighted the need for struggle with a fascinating example of nature's need for adversity.[17] In the 1980s, the United States built Biosphere 2 in an attempt to build a closed artificial ecosystem that could be self-sustaining to support life for eight human beings. The project was a failure. Why?

The trees they planted grew rapidly but then fell over. The designers did not realize that trees need wind. The wind bends the young trees, which places stress on the roots by tugging at them on the windward side and compressing the roots on the other side. The root systems expand, and the compressed cells' structure becomes stronger.

Haidt explained:

> This altered cell structure is called reaction wood or sometimes stress wood. Trees that are exposed to strong winds early in life become trees that can withstand even stronger winds when full grown. Conversely, trees that are raised in a protected greenhouse sometimes fall over from their own weight before they reach maturity.[18]

This is a powerful metaphor for kids.

The good news is, the "winds," or hard things, in kids' lives can strengthen them. The bad news is, their brains and bodies are wired to avoid doing hard things. Several of the most impactful books of the twenty-first century make this aspect of human nature clear. Dan Willingham wrote, "We are naturally curious, but we are not naturally good thinkers. In fact, we try to avoid it."[19]

Our brains tend to simplify things to make sense of the world.

Think about teaching your kids to drive. The simple act of moving a vehicle, with a steering wheel, pedals, and mirrors, will initially overwhelm their minds. But within weeks, their brains will make them believe that they can do all of that, check their hair, have a conversation, and respond to texts all at the same time.

Our brains also simplify the story of the world around us.

We simplify complex political, social, and cultural issues into sound bites because that is what we can handle. We do not want to be confronted with contradictory facts that complicate our simple narrative. This is particularly challenging when we have a world of negative narratives at our fingertips. News sources aim to grab our attention by sharing negative stories that can fit on a single phone screen[20] or suggesting we can understand crises as complex as Ukraine and Russia, Israel and Gaza, or North and South Korea in two hundred words or less.

A similar approach happens in education (more to come in chapter 5), and it has led to a "coddling" that infantilizes college students.[21]

We do the same thing to people around us. Take first impressions. In one-tenth of a second, we make assumptions about someone else's story based on their appearance.[22] Once we get to know people better, we also may reduce them to diagnoses and labels. When did we all become psychologists? Certainly, Google and AI have helped with our "training," but since when did it become okay to simplify stories with ignorant diagnoses? Sit around a middle-school lunch table, and you will hear so many different diagnoses flying around, you would think you were surrounded by psychiatrists.

Here are a few snippets of conversations I have heard, along with my interpretation in italics, with the acknowledgment that some of these disorders are real for some kids, but not to the extent that teen psychologists believe they are.

"She is such a narcissist."

Typical self-focused fourteen-year-old.

"I think I have social anxiety disorder, so my mom says I don't have to come to school on my bad days."

Middle school is hard for everyone, particularly kids who might be a bit shy. Going to school is good adversity.

"He has oppositional-defiance disorder. I don't know why the teacher thinks he will listen to her."

Middle-school boy who would rather do what he wants to do. Hold him accountable.

"He is so ADHD. He should just take some Ritalin."

Active boy for whom seven hours a day sitting quietly in plastic chairs is not an ideal learning environment.

"She has the 'tism! That is why she can't tell that we don't like her."

Socially awkward girl who might have trouble reading cues from mean girls.

Of course, my reactions to these actual comments are an oversimplification in their own way. I have taught middle-school students who have been accurately diagnosed with all these disorders (other than narcissism, which can only be diagnosed in adults), and those students have needed therapy and medication. Overdiagnosing kids who do not need therapy or treatment marginalizes the kids who do.

UNAVOIDABLE STRUGGLE

Teenagers aren't the only ones impersonating psychologists; we adults do this as well.[23] The problem is that our "diagnoses" are sometimes oversimplifying the humanity of others.[24] Certainly, some kids need therapy and medications that can support them as they move through the world, but do twelve-to-seventeen-year-olds in the United States really need over two million prescriptions for antidepressants?[25]

Demand is on the rise. Between 2016 and 2022 in the United States, the percentage of adolescents who were prescribed antidepressants increased by 43 percent.[26] In 2023, one in five adolescents reported receiving mental-health therapy and almost that many report taking prescription medication for emotions, concentration, behavior, or mental health.[27] Since 2016, diagnosed anxiety is up 61 percent, and depression is up 45 percent.[28]

A *Wall Street Journal* article titled "'Girl, Take Your Crazy Pills!' Antidepressants Recast as Hot Lifestyle Accessory" describes influencers in their twenties and thirties who evangelize for antidepressants as a way to make life better with hashtags like #livelaughlexapro and #zoloftgang. While this could reduce stigma for people who need medication, with 1.3 billion TikTok views for #antidepressants, could this create demand among kids for something that might not be necessary for some?[29] We know that influencers have emerged as significant sources of guidance for kids, with 60 percent of boys reporting that they find them inspirational[30] and 70 percent of girls saying they significantly influence their opinions.[31]

Therapy-speak and medication are everywhere, and trained and untrained people are making clinical diagnoses. When we repeatedly turn a challenge a kid faces into a disorder that requires drugs or therapy, we communicate that they do not have agency. Giving twelve-year-olds Lexapro for anxiety might be necessary to address chemical imbalances. But when we give a kid a pill to fix a problem that they might have agency to push through, how will they ever learn to deal with that issue on their own when stakes get even higher? How will they deal with the challenges that will come when they are adults?

This leads us to a few more uncomfortable yet important questions.

Could the number of kids receiving therapy and medication be inflated because some adults are seeking a shortcut to comfort? Are some of us that resistant to seeing kids experience adversity?[32]

Life is hard. If we get the privilege of living long enough, we know this is true. The longest study of happiness ever conducted confirms this. Launched in 1938, the Harvard Study of Adult Development is still tracking the lives of the original 724 participants and now three generations of more than 1,300 descendants. The current study directors wrote, "A rich life—a good life—is forged from precisely the things that make it hard."[33]

How is it possible that the good life is forged from what makes it hard?

Because deep, enduring, good things come from struggle.

And how kids view and move through struggle will depend on how the adults around them engage with it.

Illustrating this will take us back to one of the most memorable moments in my own early life—when two teachers taught me the difference between destructive struggle and productive struggle.

TAKEAWAY

"We meant well" is not an excuse.

"Our kids are well" is the goal.

Perhaps the key to being well is struggling well.

TRY THIS

Ask a few young people in your life if they agree with this finding: "A rich life—a good life—is forged from precisely the things that make it hard."

Based on their answer, ask them:

- How does that make you think about life differently?
- How does your answer affect the way you live your life?

3
BACK TO THE ABCs

When I was in first grade, art was my favorite class. I loved the smell of Elmer's glue, manila paper, and Magic Markers, and best of all, there were no words to read.

One day my art teacher, Mrs. Crabtree,[1] was passing out scissors so we could cut out heads for our Halloween witches—silver-handled scissors for the "normal" kids and green-handled scissors for the left-handed kids.

"Which ones do you use?" she asked me.

I knew I was left-handed, so I said, "The green ones."

She gave me a pair.

Now came the hard part. Which one was my left hand?

Mrs. Crabtree watched me as I mistakenly put the scissors on my right hand. She snatched them off my hand and snapped, "You are right-handed. Use these." She gave me the silver scissors.

I liked the idea of using the silver scissors because that was what everyone else used, so I tried to use them on my left hand. The construction paper wouldn't cut, so I tried what I thought was my right hand. I still couldn't make the scissors work.

I was good at basketball, kickball, and art. That was it. So recess and art had been the best parts of my school week, but now that I couldn't cut a simple circle, I wasn't sure I could say I was good at art anymore.

All the other kids were done with their witches' heads, and they were all perfect circles. Liquid frustration and shame ran hot down my cheeks. At least I was at the back of the class. Unfortunately, nothing escaped the Sauron-like eye of Mrs. Crabtree, who saw me crying. From the front of the room, she pronounced my sentence.

"Jon, if you are going to disrupt class, go to the hall."

In shame, I made myself as small as possible and tried to hide my tears from the rest of the class. I walked the length of the room to the hallway and closed the door behind me. Sitting against the cold cinder-block wall, I covered my face, my shoulders rising and falling as I unsuccessfully tried to control my sobs. I had never been kicked out of class before. Sixth graders walked by and saw me crying, deepening my humiliation.

After what seemed like hours, my first-grade teacher, Mrs. Taylor,[2] walked by.

"What is wrong?" she asked.

I could not get words to come out of my mouth as I tried to choke back my emotions. Without any words, she took me by the hand and walked me back to our first-grade classroom.

She sat down in a small, child-sized chair across from my seat, so close our knees were almost touching. She gently rested her hands on my shoulders and looked me in the eye.

"Can you tell me what happened?" she asked.

Through halting bursts, I told her.

She did not say anything in response. She enfolded me in a hug, and I was surrounded by her grandmotherly smell.

Then she did something that blew my first-grade mind. She broke teacher code. She broke adult code.

"What Mrs. Crabtree did was wrong," she stated. "She should not have done that to you."

I stopped crying, took a few deep breaths, and felt immense relief. With Mrs. Taylor looking into my eyes, I sensed there might be hope for me yet.

Mrs. Taylor saw me as more than a nuisance who was confused by scissors and could not tell the difference between easy words, letters, and numbers.

In my mind, *was* and *saw* were the same word. The letters *b* and *d* and the numbers *6* and *9* were designed by adults who just wanted to make kids' lives miserable. Because Mrs. Taylor was patient and perceptive, she eventually figured out that I was dealing with dyslexia.

The following summer, on Mrs. Taylor's recommendation, I rode my bike to a retired teacher's house every week to sit in her kitchen to go through workbook after workbook to help me learn how to navigate my dyslexia. By the time I made it to second grade, I was reading on grade level. I still had to work hard to read, but once I had read it, I did not forget it. My need for focus when reading became a gift.

Mrs. Crabtree shamed struggle.

Mrs. Taylor helped me embrace struggle. Because she saw me so clearly and believed in me anyway, I was motivated to persevere, and the struggle eventually became strength.

DESTRUCTIVE STRUGGLE VERSUS PRODUCTIVE STRUGGLE

My experiences with Mrs. Crabtree and Mrs. Taylor illustrate the difference between destructive and productive struggle. One teacher did not look closely enough to truly see her student. The other saw her student and discerned what he needed to become a better version of himself. One allowed struggle to lead to shame, removal from learning, and social isolation. The other identified a learning challenge, offered encouragement, and prescribed interventions.

I acknowledge that many kids struggle with dyslexia and other far more challenging issues than I did with Mrs. Crabtree. I was reminded of this one day in the Baylor University leadership capstone class I teach. Our group discussion prompted Divine, a student who grew up in Nigeria, to share, "When I was in grade nine, I took the blame for another student because I did not want the whole grade to get punished, and I ended up getting humiliated in front of my grade."

She offered no more details about the incident until after class, when I asked her if she would be willing to share a bit more.

"I got flogged in front of everybody," she explained.

After a stunned pause, I asked, "What do you mean *flogged*?"

My face must have registered shock because Divine was puzzled. "People in America always act that way when I tell them that."

"That is because when we hear *flogged*, we imagine someone being beaten with a whip," I said.

"Oh, sometimes they used a horsewhip," she replied matter-of-factly.

"What did they hit you with?"

"A pipe."

Horrified, I asked, "Was this the only time this happened to you?"

Divine laughed. "No, this happened all the time. If they did not know who did something, they would just punish us all."

This kind of abuse is obviously an extreme example of destructive struggle, but even if we avoid severe discipline, that doesn't mean we aren't damaging young people in other ways.

Educators hold what John Steinbeck called a "deathless power" in the way they form students for life. I would say the same is true for many adults in a student's life. We hold the power to dehumanize or humanize. Beat down or build up. Humiliate or encourage. Shame or point to joy through struggle.

Whatever your role is in a kid's life, will you be like Mrs. Crabtree or Mrs. Taylor?

Imagine a moment of struggle a kid in your life has had. Picture their frustration, which inevitably followed. Can you recall how you responded to their frustration?

In a moment of frustration, kids have two options: quit or persevere. Their tolerance for frustration is largely dependent on how adults around them present struggle. Indirectly, we are answering these questions for them:

- Is struggle positive or negative?
- Is the ability to struggle a strength or a weakness?
- Does struggle threaten my identity as "not good enough"?
- Do I lose value as a human if I struggle, because my worth is dependent on my performance?

When kids believe their worth is based on their performance, their struggle becomes destructive. If, as adults, we reinforce kids' sense that their worth is on the line, their struggle can feel dehumanizing. We can be the teacher who kicks kids out of class for struggling with scissors, or the youth coach who focuses only on wins instead of progress, or the parents who see our kids as proxies for our own success.

RESULTS VERSUS RELATIONSHIP

Let's look at a few examples of destructive and productive struggles through the lens of youth sports.[3]

When my kids were in first through sixth grade, I coached their basketball teams, which involved a one-hour practice and a one-hour game per week. On many game days I witnessed coaches yelling at refs (typically high-school volunteers) and getting extremely upset about outcomes of games. In one particularly contentious game, a coach instructed his team to foul the two best players on the opposing team, because there was no penalty for fouling. I was coaching a game on another court at the time, and I could hear the crowd's uproar about the outcome of this fourth-grade boys' basketball game.

After the games were over, I walked over to the coach who had implemented the hack-a-fourth-grader strategy.

"How does intentionally fouling their best players line up with what we are trying to teach these kids?" I asked him.

"We just win!" he proudly exclaimed. "I am the Bobby Knight of this league." For context, Bobby Knight was the legendary basketball coach at Indiana University who notoriously verbally and physically abused his players and eventually lost his job after he was captured on video choking one of his players. While this coach wasn't doing anything as egregious as Bobby Knight, he prioritized winning above all. Winning by any means was preferred to helping kids win well, develop skills, and become better people.

Kids will have a hard time becoming resilient unless we encourage struggle in the context of strong relationships. When adults do this for kids, we help them grow stronger when life's winds start blowing, much like the root systems of redwood sequoias. These trees can weigh over six tons, extend over three hundred feet into the sky, and live for thousands of years. The reason? They have root systems that are connected over miles—roots that share nutrients, bring water, and provide support. As adults, we can help form those dense networks of roots that support growth.

In a moment of discouragement, I called my brother, who was coaching basketball at the college level at the time.

"What am I doing coaching middle-school basketball?" I asked.

He did not try to cheer me up. He just said, "You are there to build relationships."

I needed the reminder.

If you have coached six-to-fourteen-year-olds, you know that the work is more about developing relationships through struggle than anything else—and that it is possible to experience joy when we struggle together, even when there is a high level of futility along the way.

I once coached a six-year-old boy we'll call Jacob, who had never played a sport before and had no idea what basketball was when the year started. He grew to love basketball because he loved playing defense, which, for him, meant literally hugging whatever boy he was assigned to defend. Each game, we had to work with the referee to help him give his opponent some room to breathe. On offense, he liked to just lie on the other end of the floor to wait until he could play defense again.

All year, we ran plays to try to get Jacob to score, which was a challenge even in practice. When a shot finally fell for him in the last game, the entire team and everyone in the gym erupted in cheers. That day, Jacob got his name written on "the Beast," a basketball that was our team's prized possession.

We kept the Beast in a duffel bag. A well-timed shake of the duffel bag gave the team a sense that the Beast was ready to emerge, but only at the end of a game or practice, when we would determine who would get their name written on the Beast. This honor went to the player who hustled the most, worked the hardest, demonstrated the most perseverance, or was a good teammate. After I wrote the name on the ball, the player would get to place a hand on the Beast while the whole team cheered loudly enough for the whole gym to know. The proud athlete whose name appeared on the Beast the most times at the end of the season got to keep it.

The Beast was just a basketball that I would buy at the beginning of each season, but it was a tool for encouraging productive struggle. It communicated the value we placed on *struggling well.*

When I got to write Jacob's name on the Beast, and he stood with his hand resting on the basketball, the first-grade cheers were deafening.

SEPARATING PERFORMANCE FROM HUMAN VALUE

Even when young people learn to persist through struggle, they can fail when they find their value exclusively in their performance.

Simone Biles, definitively the greatest gymnast and one of the greatest athletes of all time, tragically demonstrated where she had found her value after a disappointing Olympic performance. She experienced the "twisties," a condition where athletes become disoriented in the air—extremely dangerous for someone flying ten to fifteen feet off the ground while flipping and spinning at tremendous speed. As a result, she was forced to withdraw from several events.

Afterward, she posted on Twitter, "The outpouring love & support I've received has made me realize I'm more than my accomplishments and gymnastics which I never truly believed before." She had "never truly believed" that she was more than her accomplishments.

If this is true for someone as successful and confident as Simone Biles at the age of twenty-four, how does this work for a younger athlete or a six-year-old in art class? How do we help them believe that their value is more than their performance?

It's not by removing all adversity from their lives. That communicates that we do not value them enough to let them try and that their struggling is unacceptable. When we fear that they will fail—which will make us uncomfortable and them upset—we instinctively *and* tragically intervene.

Inviting kids into productive struggle communicates that they are valuable because they are human. Their worth is not dependent on whether they can cut out a witch's head, read a passage, win a basketball game, or vault twelve feet into the air. Our worth as adults is not contingent on their performance either. None of us is generically human. We are each unique with valuable gifts that we can contribute to the world, and we are allowed to be works in progress.

Kids need this deeply ingrained so they have a strong sense of it by the time they are young adults.

Meg Jay is a psychologist and expert who works with people in what she calls the "defining decade"—their twenties. It's an uncertain time in life, and one that has been overhyped, leaving people anxious that they are missing out when their lives don't resemble a TV show like *Friends* or what is curated on Instagram. She suggests taking the most interesting jobs we can in our twenties and not settling for the barista job. She encourages young people to try new things in the real world that make them more interesting and develop skills that will eventually be valuable to others.

Jay followed her own advice in her twenties by taking a job as an instructor for Outward Bound, a nonprofit that challenges kids to grow through outdoor expeditions and adventures. She developed leadership skills, character, and identity capital that allowed her to launch effectively into her future career as a psychologist.[4] Kids who get the chance to do hard things are more likely to continue to develop skills and experiences through hard things when they are older. The key: Start kids early and celebrate growth!

When we lead kids away from happiness-induced misery and toward productive struggle, we'll be leading them toward something deeper, stronger, and more durable than happiness could ever be.

Joy.

THE ABCS OF JOY

Throughout this book, I contrast joy with happiness. *Happiness* is momentary, circumstantial, self-focused pleasure. *Joy* is enduring, includes others, and is even woven into who we are. We find joy through **a**dversity that leads to **b**elonging and fuels **c**uriosity. If we want to blaze a trail for our kids to find joy, these are the ABCs. Certainly, there are other sources of joy, but adversity, belonging, and curiosity reveal and replenish our joy.

Take a moment to reflect on adversity, belonging, and curiosity. Which of those terms is least likely to be accepted as fuel for joy?

I am guessing we all agree on the word that doesn't seem to fit.

Haven't we all experienced joy through belonging? We all want to be included. In fact, we want to move beyond simply being allowed to be in a group to knowing that we belong. We are safe and comfortable and have firmly established our status within the group. We are wired for relationships. Think about what we know about student-teacher relationships, for example. A recent analysis of seventy years of studies that included 2.6 million students found that a trusting student-teacher relationship resulted in higher academic achievement, better behavior, more self-control, deeper belonging, greater motivation, and enhanced well-being.[5] When we belong, we even receive some of our status and identity from the group. Joy abounds when we not only belong but also matter. We are missed when we are not there. Others can count on us. We can count on them. That's joy, right?

What about curiosity? Have you ever found yourself completely engrossed in someone else's story? Have you ever lost track of time wondering about clouds skittering across the sky? Have you ever marveled at the way middle-school students rove in packs, curious about how they confer status on some kids and not others? We experience joy through curiosity in others, curiosity about how things work, or others' curiosity about us.

Curiosity and belonging can be mutually reinforcing. When we are curious about others, they are more likely to be curious about us. And sharing curiosity about similar things enhances belonging and leads to joy.

Conversely, haven't we all experienced a loss of joy when belonging and curiosity crumble?

The fastest way to steal middle-school kids' joy is for them to sense that they do not belong. Are we as adults really that different? We want to matter to others. When we don't feel like we do, we lose our sense of joy. Lack of belonging increases drama at work, destroys friendships, and diminishes our sense of community.

When we lose belonging, we lose joy too.

A loss of curiosity has a similar effect on joy. A kindergartner may follow his curiosity about dinosaurs enough to consider himself the greatest living expert on them, but what happens by the time he is in sixth grade? The light in his eyes is less bright as he endures the compliance-driven drudgery that school has become. Certainly, there are exceptions, but this is the case for many. We also see this in homes where kids' curiosity is anesthetized as they passively scroll through twelve-second reels, leaving no time to truly engage curiosity. Judgment that kills curiosity boils everything down to extremes, where kids pronounce "that sucks" or "that is genuinely/literally amazing."

Joy is stolen when curiosity is extinguished.

That leaves adversity. Adversity might be the key to belonging and curiosity. Imagine a life without adversity and what that would do to our sense of belonging. Don't we often figure out who matters to us—and whom we matter to—when the world feels like it is crashing in or we need someone to show up? Kids might have friends who are funny and entertaining, but they define real friendship based on who is there when things get tough. We do the same thing as adults.

Where do friendships get cemented between the ages of nine to twenty-two? Adversity plays a key role. Take a minute to think of where you made friends as a kid. Maybe these were experiences that adults organized that placed you in collective adversity, such as athletic teams, performing arts, classes, service projects, or summer camp. I also will acknowledge here that trauma—which we do not want anyone to experience, but is part of life—can establish and cement friendships. If your parents divorced, you were bullied, you lost a pet, or you were socially ostracized, who was there for you?

Where do the young people in your life find deep connection? In middle school and beyond, they increasingly will find it in friends as they all navigate the adversity they face in daily life. This is normal development and one of the primary ways they will build resilience. The denser their social connections, the more resilient they will be. When we as adults remove adversity from their lives, we are doing them a disservice, not providing the protection they actually need. Letting them build relationships through adversity will steer them toward resilience.

Young people are the "unsigned manuscripts" of adults.[6] When they reach the end of their lives, those manuscripts will be finished and signed. What part will you help young people write?

We need to help the next generation struggle well by giving them the tools they need to make progress—whether we are inviting them into productive struggle in the context of relationship with us or encouraging them to navigate adversity with their peers.

What if joy is something we embody, and happiness is just something that happens to us? Can we become joyful people by embracing adversity, belonging, and curiosity?

I have met people who seem to have figured this out. They do not just experience joy—they *are* joy. They have found the path to the good life and can help point the way for the rest of us.

TAKEAWAY

Joy is better than happiness because joy is embodied and endures. We find joy through **a**dversity that leads to **b**elonging and fuels **c**uriosity.

TRY THIS

Make a list of what brings you happiness. Then make a list of what brings you joy. How are they different?

After defining *joy* and *happiness*, ask a kid in your life to do the same exercise.

4
THE PATH TO THE GOOD LIFE

I was grading papers at our kitchen table at 11:30 p.m. when the phone rang.

"Mr. Eckert, this is Scottie Stocchero."

Scottie and his sister, Amanda, were two of my former fifth-grade students, but I had not heard from them in a few years. Now Scottie was eighteen and calling me late at night.

"Great to hear from you, Scottie. How are you doing? How is Amanda?"

Scottie paused before answering, "That is what I am calling about. Amanda is in the hospital, and the doctors do not think she will make it through the night."

Amanda had catastrophic epilepsy. As a fifth grader, her giant brown eyes were full of life, and her infectious smile seemed almost too big for her fragile body. I always had Amanda sit in the front row because her seizures were so frequent. Whenever she had one, I could place my hand under her chin to keep her head from hitting her desk while I continued to teach. The entire class came to expect this and knew it would soon pass without intervention.

While doctors had predicted that her seizures would continue to worsen over time, I wasn't ready to receive that late-night phone call from Scottie a few years later. Amanda was only sixteen years old.

I did not know what to say. The kitchen seemed incredibly dark, and the papers I had been grading two minutes earlier no longer mattered.

"She really wants you to be at her funeral," Scottie continued. "Can you come?"

Of course, I agreed.

As the doctors expected, Amanda did pass away that night. Attending Amanda's funeral was hard. I can still feel the bear hug Scottie gave me when he saw me. I can still see his mom's bloodshot eyes. Can a life be this short and also good?

I cannot find happiness in that experience.

Years removed, I do catch glimpses of joy that break through the cracks of brokenness as I reflect on it—the joy in Scottie's bear hug and the joy from the memories of Amanda loving others well. Amanda understood what it was to be physically broken at a young age. Because of her suffering, she was able to enter into others' pain *and* their joy. Her joy was not built on expectations; each day was both a challenge and a gift.

The Harvard Study of Adult Development (mentioned in chapter 2) is the longest-running study of what constitutes a good life, and it proves what most of us can attest to—that "positive relationships are essential to human well-being."[1] Amanda's life was a physical representation of this.

My joy emerges from two other sources when I remember Amanda.

First, I celebrate the freedom that she experiences on the other side of death, where seizures no longer rack her body. I am not alone in this hope, as 92 percent of Americans believe in something beyond the natural world.[2]

Second, as I grow older, I increasingly find my joy in relationships with others, especially when I have gone through adversity. I experience joy even through pain when others invite me to help carry their burdens and when they help me carry mine. As a teacher, coach, professor, and dad, I am blessed to have rich relationships with vibrant, flawed members of younger generations. Through those relationships, I experience life-giving connection, even in times of unimaginable pain.

I imagine you could say the same about your own experiences of joy amid adversity in relationships. Painful times are not about happiness at all, but we *do* get glimpses of joy, don't we? That is because happiness and joy are different.

In this chapter, we will look more closely at how they are different, before we turn to the practical ways we can steer kids toward joy, starting in the next chapter.

Let's begin with the acknowledgment that you and I want the best for the young people around us—that is why you are reading this book. We want to do everything we can to put them on a path to a good life.

But if I asked you to pinpoint what exactly a "good life" is, that might be tougher to answer, wouldn't it?

A BRIEF LOOK AT THE GOOD LIFE

Robert Waldinger and Marc Schulz, the researchers behind the Harvard Study of Adult Development, wrote a book based on the study called *The Good Life*. In short, they found that a good life is built on hard things, and it requires relationships.[3] This aligns well with Aristotle's view of a good life built on the pursuit of virtue for communal flourishing, *eudaimonia* (for non-Greek scholars like me, that is pronounced "yoo-day-MOH-nee-uh").[4]

Simply put, the good life is built on love. This might sound like an oversimplification, but nearly every world religion and everyone's lived experience points to love as the source of flourishing.

Jewish law and Christian faith are built on love, which is summarized in the quote, "The whole law is fulfilled in one word: 'You shall love your neighbor as yourself.'"[5] In the thirteenth century, Thomas Aquinas echoed this, writing that love is "to will the good of the other."[6]

Hindus use the word *bhakti*, which means "boundless, unconditional love" of others. Tibetans use the word *tsewa*, which means "love" and is the "source of all goodness in the world." And Buddhists use the word *metta* to mean an "unselfish love for all beings."

Love is the source of transformational social and political movements. Take, for example, Martin Luther King Jr.'s claim that "love is ultimately the only answer to [humanity's] problems."[7]

Another ancient word that might be helpful is *shalom*, a Hebrew word that is usually translated as "peace" and, to modern ears, sounds like freedom from trouble. *Shalom*, however, refers to "absolute wholeness—full, harmonious, joyful, flourishing life."[8] Isn't this what every religion, every community, and every human being wants—a full, harmonious, flourishing life?

So we might say that "the good life" is a life of communal flourishing and *shalom* grounded in love. But how many of us in the modern world are pursuing this?

Harvard University and Baylor University have partnered in a study of what flourishing looks like around the world in a survey of over two hundred thousand people in countries that represent 64 percent of the world's population. The researchers defined *flourishing* as "the relative attainment of a state in which all aspects of a person's life are good, including the contexts in which that person lives."[9]

They differentiate *well-being* from *flourishing* by associating well-being primarily with the individual and flourishing with the community and environment.[10] In other words, flourishing requires others. Bestselling author Dan Coyle tells us that "community" means "shared gifts." We do not build community; we awaken community. Having grown up in Alaska, he is convinced that we need a certain amount of suffering to effectively build flourishing communities.[11]

Maybe that is why in countries where there has been a primary emphasis on material well-being, like the United States and Japan, there are lower levels of flourishing. (The U.S. was in the bottom half of countries, and Japan was the lowest scoring country.)

Tyler VanderWeele, one of the lead researchers from Harvard, explained why this might be the case. "I tend to think you end up getting what you value most. When a society is oriented toward economic gain, you will be moderately successful, but not if it's done at the expense of meaning and community."[12]

What do we value most for our kids? I don't think it is economic gain *at the expense* of meaning and community.

What makes a good life?

I don't think it is happiness. I think it is joy.

Happiness is circumstantial, is self-focused, and withers in struggle.

We will not find this somewhat-negative definition in a dictionary, Google search, or AI query. People from Confucius to Aristotle to Oprah Winfrey cannot agree on the meaning of *happiness*. I am suggesting that we find this definition—as well as the one that follows—in the lives lived around us.

Joy is the overflow of enduring love and gratitude for others, and it emerges through struggle.

Here's one other way to think of this. Our circumstances often dictate happiness—think, "That makes me happy." An external force influences happiness. Joy comes from something deep within and between us. When I say, "I am joyful," I am making a statement that I am embodying joy, and my joy wells up from some deeper connection to the world and others.

JOY THROUGH STRUGGLE

We said in the last chapter that if we do not give our students a chance to struggle, then we rob them of the chance to develop new skills and resilience. Now we will look at something else we rob them of when we do this: true joy.

In a world of air-conditioning, Uber Eats, and virtual reality, where comfort seems to be life's goal, it is possible for some kids to grow up with the notion that struggle can be avoided. And yet, when young people are on the other side of productive struggle, they admit that they consider it to be worthwhile, even joyful.

At the Baylor Center for School Leadership, we asked thirty-eight thousand students from Australia, Cambodia, Canada, Indonesia, and the United States how much they agree with the statement, "I experience joy by doing hard things in this class." Over 65 percent of students "agreed" or "strongly agreed."

For clarity, "doing hard things" in this discussion does not mean enduring trauma like the abuse Divine described in chapter 3. I do not wish trauma on anyone. Here I am addressing the benefits young people can gain from facing adversity—instances where they can work hard collectively toward a goal that initially feels out of reach.

This can happen in classrooms, like the students we surveyed who experienced joy by doing hard things. It also can happen when unavoidable tragedy strikes, as it did in Augusta, Georgia, in 2024.

Hurricane Helene battered the town with hundred-mile-per-hour winds, uprooting massive pine trees, snapping them off "like spears," and hurling them into people's homes. Afterward, residents had no running water for five days. Schools were flooded and lost power, keeping them closed for repair for weeks. The hurricane was a traumatic event for Augusta and many other communities.

The home of a first grader named Jude[13] survived the storm, but his family's cars did not, and his relatives' homes were destroyed. To reconnect with the rest of his family at a meeting point on the street, they needed to climb through pine trees for a quarter mile. Jude cried the whole way. When they eventually drove back days later, Jude covered his eyes and told his mom that it was "too hard to look."

Jude's mom was worried about how he might react when he returned to school. But, because of diligent work crews, when Jude saw it for the first time after the hurricane, he exclaimed, "Oh Mom, it's really normal here! I'm so glad to be here." It was a sentiment shared by many students and a reward to the educators and staff who had spent countless hours restoring the building.

"In some ways, the kids have handled these trying circumstances better than the adults," Kellie House, a teacher at Jude's school, observed. They demonstrated resilience and a "natural inclination" to find hope, "always looking for the good." Kellie's own kids were "thrilled" to spend time volunteering with their dad to help support people and make homes livable. Her kids found joy through serving and described it as a "ministry almost to yourself when serving."

We do not develop resilience because we have a backbone that is already strong; we develop resilience by building the muscles around the backbone as we do hard things.[14] In this case, that muscle development might have been literal as well as figurative, but I am certain those students will remember and appreciate more from that school year than any other because of what they went through together.

Here was a violent, devastating event no one could control and no one wanted. But even a natural disaster like this can provide opportunities for joy to emerge through adversity by transforming the everyday aspects of life that we often take for granted into a collective goal.

JOY WITH OTHERS

The philosopher John Stuart Mill wrote, "Those only are happy . . . who have their minds fixed on some object other than their own happiness."[15] Researchers have confirmed this notion,[16] showing that excessive focus on our own happiness does not lead to joy,[17] and many of us sense this as well.

If I want to move to a more joyful state, I need to shift my thoughts to others.

Can I experience joy apart from others? Certainly. I have experienced joyful points of connection to nature when sitting by the ocean, watching the Texas sun paint the sky every shade from purple to orange. I have experienced joy when hearing the breeze blowing through shimmering aspen leaves in the mountains or smelling homemade bread that reminds me of my childhood. Those moments connect to something bigger or a memory of something I treasure. I am still connecting to someone or something in a transcendent way.

My greatest joys, however, are experienced with others—wins, graduations, marriages, births, or moments of insights.

We see this on a societal level as well as an individual one. In the United States, societal shifts demonstrate a move away from thinking of "we" and a move toward "I" since the 1960s.[18] The data in chapter 1 show that loneliness is on the rise—not a surprising result of moving away from "we." "I" might lead to happiness and some form of well-being, but "we" is more likely to lead to joy and flourishing.

Our joy is complete when it is for and with others.

As I watched the finals of the women's long jump at the Paris Olympic Games in 2024, Tara Davis-Woodhall won the gold medal. Her husband, Hunter Woodhall, wore a "Team Tara" T-shirt, radiating joy. Tara ran to the stands and jumped into his arms as he yelled, "You are the Olympic champion!" His joy was entirely for her.

Several weeks later in Paris, Hunter won the gold in the 400 meters, and it was his turn to run to the stands and jump into Tara's arms. Her joy was complete in his success.

What I did not realize when I first watched the clip of Tara jumping into Hunter's arms was that he was a Paralympian. Having lost his legs when he was eleven months old, he used running blades to race.

When we see athletes competing at the Olympics, we do not see all the struggle that got them to that level. We think of events like the 400 meters and the long jump as individual events performed by superhuman athletes. We do not see the years of suffering, the perseverance, and the people who made their success possible.

We can find some level of happiness from easy wins that we achieve by ourselves—a Ping-Pong victory, a good grade in a class that is not challenging, or a chance to cross a simple task off a to-do list—but those experiences do not lead to enduring joy. The amount we struggle has a direct relationship with how much joy we experience; the depth of our struggle often determines the peak of our joy.

And as creatures built for relationships, joy is magnified when we live life *for* and *with* others. Neither Hunter's nor Tara's joy would have been as great without struggle. Maybe even more importantly, their joy required each other.

JOY AMID SUFFERING

Jensen Huang is the cofounder and CEO of Nvidia, a computer chip company worth trillions of dollars. Onstage at Stanford University, his alma mater, Huang told students, "I wish upon you ample doses of pain and suffering." As someone who once attended a boarding school in rural Kentucky, where he was bullied and subjected to every possible Asian racial slur, Huang is acquainted with suffering. He went on to explain that "greatness comes from character. And character isn't formed out of smart people. It's formed out of people who suffered."[19]

Do you agree with him?

As I've written earlier, I do not wish trauma on anyone. *And* I do think that we all can grow through adversity.

Whether we want to experience adversity or not, we learn over a lifetime that pain is a part of life—but so is joy.

Much of the way we respond to adversity depends on our mindset. Some of the most joyful people I know have also suffered more than I can imagine. The flip side of that coin? Many of the most miserable people I know choose to be miserable. When we focus exclusively on our own pain, a childish but often natural response, we do not experience the joy that comes from realizing how that pain might be shaping us to better walk alongside others.

I never have been, nor will I ever be, an Olympic athlete—this is still a sad realization for me. If you see me walking, you might wonder, *What is going on with the way he walks?* My left leg bows out. Since I now live in Texas, I would love to claim this is from my rugged past as a cowboy and too many years spent on horseback. Sadly, I do not even own a pair of boots, a belt buckle, or a cowboy hat.

After growing up in Indiana and playing basketball regularly for almost forty years, two knee surgeries in quick succession left the inner part of my left knee without any cartilage. Now the femur and tibia grind together on each step. Every three months, a doctor gives me a cortisone shot that allows me to tolerate the pain—and postpones the doctor replacing bone with titanium, at least for a while longer.

My pain is a daily reminder of what will not be—no pain-free running, much less an Olympic or NBA future. I focus, instead, on lifting weights, playing pickleball, biking, and shooting baskets occasionally—and I am grateful. Not being able to do whatever I want makes me grateful for things that are possible. Not being able to play basketball makes me grateful for the forty years I did play. The stark contrast increases the joy of my memories. Riding my bike, even my stationary one, elicits joy because I am still able to be active.

I might not be able to run alongside others anymore, but I can still walk despite a limp. In fact, maybe I can walk alongside others better because of that limp.

Hunter Woodhall does not have legs, and he runs faster than I ever could. Undoubtedly, he experiences joy even through the pain that comes from pushing his body to its limit; his joy might be greater because of the challenges he has overcome.

We do not need to minimize our challenges because others have greater challenges. My knee does not hurt any less because Hunter Woodhall does not have legs. My knee, however, is a throbbing reminder that there is suffering in the world *and* that there is joy. Frequently, suffering and joy are linked.

As we reflect on life experiences, we can have more joy in realizing how precious and fleeting life is. If we only focus on our happiness in a moment, then we only feel our limitations and try to cling to the moment. We miss joy.

JOY + STRUGGLE = NOT MISERABLE

I am suggesting that sometimes being miserable is a choice. Think of some of the most joyful people you know, especially older people. Has everything gone well for them? Are they joyful because their circumstances are just better than yours?

Some of the most joyful people I know are the ones who have suffered the most—they are the opposite of miserable. Erik Ellefsen is one of those people for me, for many of his past students, and for thousands of educators impacting students around the world.

When Erik was thirty-two, he started getting black spots in his vision and eventually was diagnosed with multiple myeloma. Doctors expected him to live for only two to five more years. He immediately started chemotherapy and had a bone marrow transplant. He and his wife would never be able to have their own kids because of his treatments, and they relocated from Chicago to California to be closer to her family in case she was widowed. Because of his lower energy levels, Erik could no longer work as a high-school principal and instead took a job as a college counselor at a high school.

Before that diagnosis, Erik and I had big dreams of bringing joy to the profession that makes all others possible: education. We started teaching outside of Chicago at about the same time a few miles apart from each other. We parted ways for doctoral work—Vanderbilt University for me, Boston University for him. At least once a month, we would talk on the phone for two to three hours about what we were learning in our programs and what we might be able to do when we completed our degrees.

Our dreams did not stop after his diagnosis.

Erik has now been through two bone marrow transplants, four CAR T-cell transplants, and over one hundred bone marrow biopsies. He has been on immunotherapy or chemotherapy for eighteen years. We pray that each new experimental treatment—everything he does is experimental because all the treatments he has been on for the last ten years did not exist when he was diagnosed—will give him another year so researchers can find the next treatment.

Erik has not been healed. He has been sick more than anyone I know, has neuropathy in his hands and feet, and has lost 25 percent of his body mass. His best day is probably worse than my worst one. Because he never knows if he will have the energy or if he will be alive, his work is never about him.

Before his diagnosis, Erik was an outstanding leader who was confident to the point of cocky about his ability to lead a great school. After his diagnosis, he became confidently humble and started putting smart, passionate people together to do better work. He is the best person I know for building community and can count thousands of friends in countries all over the world. He is also the best friend I have ever had. We now get to work together at the Baylor Center for School Leadership, where he can work remotely from California as our director of networks and improvement.

Erik just turned fifty. Some people stop celebrating birthdays when they get to ages like fifty. Not Erik. He has been an educator for almost thirty years now. Over half of those years came after he was not supposed to be on this earth anymore.

Relationships are what give him life. He leads Zoom sessions with leaders from around the world from the hospital when he is getting treatment. He goes to weddings of forner students in India, and last year, he attended my son's wedding with "uncle" status—conferred on those friends whom we chose to make our family. Our family has been praying for Erik for the past eighteen years—for as long as our son can remember.

Because of Erik, our kids have learned the joy of carrying others' burdens. We do a disservice to our kids when we act as if struggle does not exist. This lie leads them to believe that struggle can be avoided, and it keeps them from building the muscles that will allow them to meet adversity that will come later, when we can no longer shelter them.

Much of Erik's journey has not been happy. But supporting him as he supports others, including my family, has been joyful. Can the good life be good even when it is hard? For me, Erik is evidence that both can be true.

We find joy not when we pursue happiness but when we struggle well together. Along the way to a good life, we build each other up—especially our kids.

TAKEAWAY

Happiness withers in struggle. Joy emerges through struggle. By embodying joy, we can point the next generation toward the good life.

TRY THIS

Make a list of the most joyful people you know. What do they have in common?

Ask a few young people in your life to do the same. Are you on their list? If not, how can you tap more deeply into joy?

PART 2

LIFE IS HARD *AND* JOYFUL

After observing students for thirty years and working alongside educators around the world, I see significant course corrections needed to reduce our emphasis on happiness and move toward the joy that fuels well-lived lives.

The path forward does not involve toxic positivity; life is hard *and* joyful. Kids need to move toward flourishing, experiencing the joy that emerges through adversity.

Anyone who spends time with young people can cultivate the conditions for this, and the "Flourishing Community" graphic on the following page provides a framework for how I (and my colleagues at the Baylor Center for School Leadership) see this working.

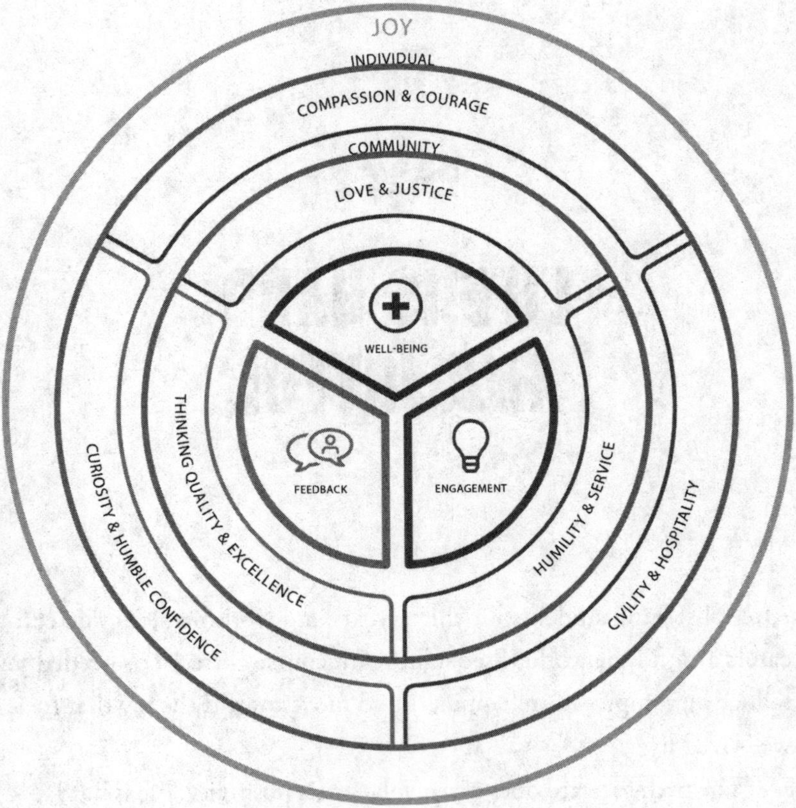

Everything in the framework flows from and should result in joy, which is why the model is bounded by joy.

At the center are three wedges:

- **WELL-BEING:** If we prioritize well-being, a community of love and justice can be built, and compassion and courage can be developed in individuals.
- **ENGAGEMENT:** If each kid is meaningfully engaged, communities of humility and service will be established, populated by civil and hospitable individuals.

- **FEEDBACK:** If each kid is well and engaged, then feedback is possible. Providing purpose-driven wisdom and guidance for growth will cultivate communities marked by thinking quality and excellence, filled with individuals who are confidently humble and curious.

In short, this is a visual for building flourishing communities through *feedback*, *engagement*, and *well-being* (FEW) for joy. The rest of the book builds on this framework.

Some will push back on these virtues, arguing that virtues represent values that are being forced on others. Do we want to live in a world without these virtues, though? Wouldn't the world be a much more joyful place with more compassion, courage, civility, hospitality, curiosity, and humble confidence? I believe this is possible.

It will take a group of gritty optimists who believe we can become more of who we are meant to be based on evidence and experience. Collectively, we can help the individuals around us flourish and lead a generation that could be liberated by joy.

5
KIDS GROW UP BY DOING HARD THINGS

What do you do when you see kids struggling with something that is hard?

What if the kids are your own?

Consider what you would do in each of these scenarios.

ELEMENTARY SCHOOL: Your kid does not want to go to school because other kids are unkind, and the teacher is unfair.

MIDDLE SCHOOL: Other kids are making fun of your kid for not having a phone or social media. She is missing out on social opportunities.

HIGH SCHOOL/COLLEGE: Your kid is caught using AI to write an essay that was supposed to be done on his own. He might not pass the class, which means he would have to repeat it.

Each of these situations is a great opportunity for meaningful conversations with our kids. Our first step shouldn't be to intervene with teachers but to coach our kids. We should step in only when it's absolutely necessary. These hard moments are great chances for our kids to grow up.

The elementary-school student needs to learn how to persevere through conflict, how to relate to difficult people, and how to navigate recess. If he doesn't learn this in elementary school, how will he become a functional adolescent and adult? While recess stakes seem high to the elementary student, the real-world stakes that lie ahead are much higher. Successful navigation of future challenges requires elementary conflict as a training ground.

The middle schooler needs to learn that you as a parent are not trying to raise her to be like other kids. She is uniquely designed to be exactly who she is. Yes, she will likely miss out on some social opportunities to sit in a basement with other kids, all of them staring at their own screens in the same location. But she still has many opportunities for meaningful connection available to her. How can you help her engage in the real world? I am increasingly convinced that having eyes up and out instead of focused on a screen will increase the social skills of all middle-school kids.

To understand the dilemma for the high-school student, perhaps a college student can shed some light. Nathan Bachman, a current student of mine at Baylor, sees many other students give in to the temptation to use AI for assignments. He described sitting in the library on a Friday night deliberating whether to use AI to finish an assignment quickly to free up the evening for friends or to grind out the assignment on his own and actually learn the content.

"Most students are aware of the long-term negative ramifications," he said. "However, the short-term return conceals the long-run costs." A good grade with additional free time more than outweighs the long-term benefit of actually learning something. AI supports productivity, not necessarily learning.

He added, "AI-powered tools provide a prescription for problem-solving like never before, in the form of a deadly opiate."

Failing a class might be the best thing that can happen to a fifteen-year-old kid to help him understand the benefit of learning, and more importantly, the value of integrity. While AI holds tremendous potential, if not used intentionally and with integrity, it could be one of the greatest challenges we face in helping kids do hard things.

In a recent study from MIT, researchers found that college students who used ChatGPT to help them write essays in response to provocative questions produced "statistically homogenous essays," and their brain activity was localized and poorly coordinated. Minutes after completing their essays, only 17 percent could remember a single sentence of them.[1]

In this chapter, we will look at what happens when young people are—and are not—given the opportunity to grow up. We also will explore the "gritty optimism" that trains kids to struggle well, fostering the kind of growth and perseverance they will need for life.

Let's start by visiting two different learning environments and considering what each one reveals about various mindsets around struggling.

THE FREE: INSIDE AND OUT

Entering a prison, even as a visitor, is a sobering experience. Clouds floated freely across the sky as two colleagues and I visited a juvenile detention center surrounded by high fences topped with razor wire. After making our way through security and numerous locked doors, we reached the dormitories housing violent youth offenders. Several kids were permitted to come out of their cells only while wearing shackles. Others were educated inside their rooms, which looked more like prison cells than dorm rooms.

In the block for less-violent offenders, we entered an English classroom, where seven boys shuffled into class. After their teacher, Ms. Parks, led a fifteen-minute discussion about agriculture, we headed out to an on-site garden with a guard.

Clearly happy to be outside, the students used a tiller, hoes, and other tools to weed the rows of potatoes, onions, watermelons, radishes, and cucumbers. One student found a barely emerging cucumber and, succumbing to his desire for instant gratification, took a bite—which he immediately spat out.

"We lose about 90 percent of the produce to instant gratification," a teacher supervising the garden shared. "Kids impulsively pull up plants or try to eat the fruits and vegetables before they are ripe. It's a generational issue."

We returned from the garden to Ms. Parks' next class—a class that consisted of only one student because he was thirteen and the youngest student at the detention center.

He told Ms. Parks he was refusing to do things in detention. When she asked why, he explained, "I like it here better than out 'in the free' [outside the detention center]. If I stay here long enough, I can get out and just get a job."

I cannot imagine how bad life "in the free" must have been for this student.

How do parents and educators create opportunities for young people to struggle well so they don't end up going to school behind razor wire?

Another school in Memphis, Tennessee, has some answers.

New Hope is a school that has served students age three through sixth grade for the past three decades. Located in a fresh food desert, the students care for land that was donated to the school by Habitat for

Humanity. New Hope has cultivated one and a half acres of land for a farm, where students grow fruits and vegetables they make available to the community on Fridays.

When I asked Lionel Cable, New Hope's leader, if they lose a lot of produce due to the impulsive need for instant gratification of this generation, he seemed surprised.

In a quietly confident voice, he responded, "We don't have that issue, because the students know that they are growing the food for their community."

A self-focused desire for instant gratification diminishes when students have the objective of welcoming others into the literal and figurative fruit of their labors. This tangible act of hospitality extends to all aspects of New Hope's culture.

Former student Joi Taylor Johnson, New Hope's current advancement director, said, "New Hope stuck with me even after I graduated from sixth grade." Every student who completes sixth grade at New Hope is eligible for an $8,500 scholarship, which allows them to attend an independent school of their choosing. There is also an office of student support to help each student graduate from high school and get to college. New Hope has a 99.9 percent high-school graduation rate as well as a 99.9 percent college placement rate.

Students at New Hope received support for struggling well, and they witnessed the positive impact their efforts had on their community.

Ms. Parks helped her students' well-being through nearly miraculous intervention, guiding them into new behaviors and possibilities in life.

Both have evidence that kids can be more of who they are meant to be—evidence that can help kids move beyond pessimism and naïve optimism to gritty optimism.

THREE MINDSET OPTIONS

Adults and kids have three options for viewing the world:

1. **PESSIMISM:** No matter what we do, the future is bleak and will remain that way.
2. **NAÏVE OPTIMISM:** Things will get better. We do not know how, but the future will improve.
3. **GRITTY OPTIMISM:** Grounded in evidence, we know things can be better even if the future is hard.

If you sometimes find yourself in the first category, you're not alone. Only 30 percent of Americans believe that the next generation will be better off than the last.[2] This pessimism, however, runs counter to decades of evidence.

Since the nineteenth century, worldwide life expectancy has more than doubled,[3] and the percentage of children living past the age of five has increased from 50 to 96 percent.[4] The percentage of people living in extreme poverty has dropped from 90 percent to less than 10 percent.[5] In a survey of people in 142 countries, more people are living better lives than before. Globally, the number of people saying they are suffering is down to 7 percent, tying the lowest level since 2004.[6]

If these facts represent reality, then why don't we feel that the world is getting better?

Because our negativity bias draws our attention to threats. We spend much of our lives in a world built on algorithms that attempt to capture our attention. In fact, the previous 142-country survey captured the sense of pessimism in the United States and Canada, where the number of people reporting they were thriving dropped significantly between 2007 and 2024—from 67 to 49 percent.[7]

Slipping into a pessimistic mindset is one of the easiest things we can do. But when we do this, we are forgetting that we have agency in our world—especially when hard things happen. Our negative feelings do not have to be permanent, pervasive, or outside of our control; instead, these feelings can be temporary, local, and within our control.[8]

To overcome a world designed to take advantage of our negativity bias, we need to purposefully cultivate gritty optimism. We'll spend the rest of this chapter unpacking what that means by contrasting it with naïve optimism.

NAÏVE OPTIMISM

Part of being a child is being naïve. A naïve toddler who is experiencing things like ice cream, walking, or a pool for the first time is beautiful. A naïve twenty-eight-year-old living in his mom's basement experiencing life exclusively through the blue light of screens is not.

As adults, we need to welcome kids into a world of responsibility *and* joy. A colleague recently shared a conversation he had with his child's babysitter, who told him, "I hate adulting."

His response to her was, "There has never been a better time to be an adult. We have more conveniences, supports, and opportunities to shape our lives than ever before."

He wasn't wrong.

But the babysitter is not alone in hating adulting. The statistics on kids not growing up are daunting, and the "failure to launch" narrative is now a familiar one. While mental health and economic challenges play a role, the reality is striking. More than half of American eighteen-to-twenty-four-year-olds still live with their parents. That number is one in three for eighteen-to-thirty-four-year-olds.[9]

What is the key to raising kids who want to grow up and launch? Could it be about shifting from naïve optimism to gritty optimism? Many kids believe they can be more, but they lack evidence that proves more is possible.

Naïve optimism is not altogether a bad thing: It can launch careers or convince us we can raise kids effectively. But unfortunately, the world can take a sledgehammer to naïve optimism.

As a beginning teacher, I thought I was going to change the world one fifth-grade class at a time. My first field trip should have shaken my confidence.

As our bus was heading down the Eisenhower Expressway to downtown Chicago, I noticed one of my toughest boys looking a bit green.

"Mr. Eckert, I don't feel so good," he moaned.

Thinking quickly, I yelled, "Stick your head out the window."

The bus was moving at fifty-five miles per hour, and many windows were open. When the greenish student complied, the contents of his stomach exited the window—and promptly reentered the bus on the next three rows of students.

Suffice it to say, several students had a rough day at the Field Museum.

Even after this remarkably unfortunate experience, I still believed I could be a great teacher because of my naïve optimism. It truly can be a gift as we persevere through mistake after mistake, both as professionals and parents.

My wife and I attended our first parent-teacher conference when our oldest child was in kindergarten. Student self-portraits lined the hallway—precious drawings of smiling kids surrounded by colorful images of families, homes, and pets. A small sign announced that these were the students in their favorite places. At the bottom right—well below an adult's line of sight, where savvy teachers know to put the less-than-exemplary work—my wife and I saw some artwork that was not like the others.

The artist had used a black crayon almost exclusively. The kid's eyes looked deranged, and he appeared to be in some type of coffin. Off to the side was a form that resembled fetal Voldemort in the eighth Harry Potter movie.

The kid who created this piece must be emotionally disturbed, I thought, with pity for his parents.

Then my wife and I saw the name. *Ben E. E* as in *Eckert*.

This was our offspring, our genetic contribution to the world. How were we qualified to raise this apparently emotionally unstable kid, let alone his younger sisters back at our apartment?

Later that night, we asked Ben about his self-portrait.

"That is me in my bed," he explained.

We asked him who the fetal Voldemort was.

"Oh, that is Sarah"—his sister with whom he shared a room. To this day, we are not sure she has fully forgiven him for his depiction of her.

This was not an isolated incident of awkwardness in parent-teacher conferences. Several years later, a fifth-grade teacher let us know that our youngest daughter, Grace, liked to bleat like a goat in class.

Bad management of bus illness, disturbing art, and in-class goat bleating may not seem like significant challenges, but they feel like it in the moment. Certainly, we all have experienced far greater challenges than these—times when reality crushed our idealized selves and caused us to question our ability to navigate the world.

If I had only naïve optimism to fuel my parenting and teaching, I eventually would have withered in the face of shame.

While naïve optimism is often necessary to get us started, gritty optimism is what keeps us going.

GRITTY OPTIMISM

Naïve optimism involves a general sense of hope. Gritty optimism is the belief that we can become more of who we are meant to be *based on evidence and experience*. We are more open to different possibilities because we have seen others become better versions of themselves and seen ourselves grow.

Although Ben's artistic talent never developed much past black crayons, my wife and I have seen him grow so much in other areas. He recently graduated from college with four majors; art was not one of them. As a senior in high school, Grace no longer bleats like a goat—at least not in class. Parents and educators build gritty optimism when they repeatedly see kids growing up and becoming more than they imagined they could be. Kids build it as well as they prove to themselves they can do what once felt out of reach.

We can think of gritty optimism as "optimism turned rational," because we are staking our hope in actual experience and evidence—the kind that demonstrates how joy can emerge in hard times.

Grit is the power of passion and perseverance[10] to become more of who we are created to be. It is something most of us desire but do not really want to go through the process of developing, because it involves discomfort and pushing through embarrassing moments. Over the past decade, grit has sometimes been conflated with compliance—simply persevering through drudgery. That, however, misses the passion component of grit, which animates perseverance.

Moving from perseverance to passion requires optimism.

Optimism is built on the expectation that the future will be positive even if it is hard. Thomas Aquinas once described hope, which is closely related to optimism, as a "future good" that might be "difficult but possible to attain."[11]

Difficult but possible. How often is a phrase like that driving us?

The future good that you and your kids need is not based on naïve optimism that will wilt whenever you are confronted with a challenge. No, it requires gritty optimism that will fuel the belief that young people can become more of who they are created to be.

MODELING AND TEACHING GRITTY OPTIMISM

If we believe that well-being is freedom from struggle, we cannot develop gritty optimism—and it's unlikely the kids around us will.

When you feel you are lacking gritty optimism as a parent or educator, remind yourself of a few truths:

- Young people learn through productive struggle.
- It is an act of love for you to lead them into that productive struggle.
- Productive struggle results in agency that leads to growth.
- Joy is possible, even if the future is hard.

As you settle into this mindset, start reframing kids' approaches to struggle as something that is okay, manageable, necessary, and even desirable, because it helps them become more of who they are meant to be.

Then start cultivating gritty optimism that leads to joy—both in yourself and in them—by doing the following three things.

1. TELL THEM THE TRUTH ABOUT WHO THEY ARE BECOMING.

Whenever we tell kids they can be anything they want to be, we are lying to them. Gritty optimism requires us to tell them the truth about who we see them becoming. That is different from who we want them to be, who we wish we would have been as kids, or who we think they want to be. While it is tempting to tell kids what we think they want to hear because we're worried about shutting them down or popping their self-esteem balloons, that doesn't set them up for success.

Kids cannot become anything they want to be. Knowing this is helpful because having an infinite number of choices can be paralyzing.[12]

Eliminating options like "graphic designer" or "portrait artist" from Ben's list of future occupations was a gift; it led him to focus on his actual talents and interests. He is brilliant at solving mathematical problems, connecting with people, and spreading exuberant joy as an enthusiast. Over the past seventeen years, he has become more of who he is created to be as he has developed skills that will allow him to serve others.[13]

Reality narrows options by closing doors, and that is a blessing.

2. INSTILL IN THEM A SENSE OF AGENCY.

Agency is the belief that we have control over our lives, and it allows us to grow through challenges. We are not bystanders waiting for a future that will happen to us. We can actively shape who we will become.

Martin Seligman, the father of positive psychology, described agency as a "psychological superpower" because it allows us to persist and do hard things. More of us need this superpower.

Angela Duckworth, the world's foremost expert on grit, has stated, "If we want this young generation to feel more optimistic about the future and their futures, we need to create opportunities where they can make a difference that, for themselves, is evidence that they're not helpless."[14]

To develop agency, kids need to see progress toward a goal. If they can stack small wins on the way to bigger wins, they will develop agency.

We don't climb Mount Everest on a whim. For a middle schooler, Mount Everest might be making the basketball team. A parent recently told me, "My son decided to go out for the basketball team. He got home from the tryout and told me, 'I think I should make the team. I gave one hundred percent and tried as hard as I could.'" When he did not make the team, he was surprised.

What was missing in this kid's formula for success?

All the days, weeks, and years leading up to the tryout, he needed to stack small wins—making ten free throws in a row, working on defensive slides, and keeping his eyes up while doing ball-handling drills. Giving 100 percent effort at a tryout does not mean much if there has not been 100 percent effort in the weeks prior.

Helping our kids see the progress they are making builds motivation to continue to improve. The harder the challenge, and the more they stack wins, the more likely they are to develop greater agency that might lead to passion.

While passion plays a role in gritty optimism, it is not helpful to advise kids simply to "follow their passions." If they followed their twelve-year-old passions, we would have a lot of people trying to make a career out of playing video games.

Young people need the opportunity to develop competence that leads to confidence, which might eventually become passion. Instead of following unformed, ill-defined passions, kids need to work at developing skills that could benefit others, which will build in them a sense of agency.

3. HELP THEM UNDERSTAND PURPOSE.

"Why do we need to learn this?" is kryptonite in classrooms around the world—if it goes unanswered. Lack of purpose erodes agency. To instill a sense of purpose, we can help our kids understand how they are uniquely created and encourage them to do hard things and stack small wins.

We can start having these conversations very early, laying the foundation for perseverance into adolescence and young adulthood. What are hard things a four-year-old has to do? Eating vegetables, following rules for games, identifying numbers and letters, figuring out how to be kind, and getting along with a sibling. Navigating each of these things early in life leads a child to become a better adult. They just need adults to help them see the underlying purpose and celebrate progress.

Now consider a school example. Typically, high-school math classrooms echo with plaintive cries of "When am I ever going to use this?" Calculus seems especially dubious, but I have seen a classroom filled with more than thirty seniors digging deeply into Calculus III. If you are like me and do not know what Calculus III entails, then you would have a difficult time explaining why it needs to be learned. In this New York City classroom, however, students were engaged in solving equations using symbols that were foreign to me.

What impressed me most was that I could not even find the teacher at first. She was kneeling beside the desk of one of her students, while other students were working together. She had created a classroom culture where students believed they could do hard things, and maybe more importantly, that they could help their peers do hard things. Her students' success was not dependent on her inspiration. Their success depended on their sense of purpose-driven gritty optimism.

Throughout the period, students were using agency to stack small wins that would lead to the bigger win of conquering Calculus III—all for the purpose of developing skills that could be valuable to others someday.

TURTLES, NOT CRABS

We can know all this and be committed to cultivating gritty optimism—and yet pessimism can still seep in. To encourage you to combat this, I will use a phrase I have told thousands of adults: "Be a turtle, not a crab."

Most of them were scratching their heads at first too.

A sociologist once described elementary schools as being "crab bucket cultures."[15] If you've ever seen a bucket full of crabs, you know you do not need a lid to keep the crabs in the bucket. Although they can climb out, they rarely do, because when one crab begins to climb up the side of the bucket, the other crabs drag it back down.

"Crab bucket culture" develops when we drag down a colleague, parent, or kid when they are recognized for doing something well. When a teacher is recognized as the "Teacher of the Year," her colleagues mutter things like this:

"She gets all the extra resources."

"She does not get the tough kids."

Or, "I'd like to see what she would do with the parents of my students."

Instead of celebrating each other's wins, they diminish them.

Parents, we do this when we see other people's kids doing amazing things. We tear others down because we feel the insecurity that comes from our own parenting uncertainty. Other kids look more successful than ours, so we defensively tear others down.

"She is just naturally talented. Things are easy for her."

"If we could afford travel ball, our kid would have made that team."

"That kid is popular only because of who her mom knows."

This pessimism is corrosive to gritty optimism and bad for anyone listening to us. We need to stop being crabs! Instead, we need to be more like turtles.

Sea turtles bury their eggs in the sand. When the eggs begin to crack, the stronger sea turtles emerge first and help the weaker ones crack their shells. The stronger turtles then use their flippers to push the others up and out of the hole, as they make the harrowing journey to the sea.[16]

We need more turtles in this world. Here are a few examples of what a turtle looks like.

At a memorial service for their father, a ten-year-old, sixteen-year-old, and eighteen-year-old shared how their dad had been their fiercest advocate. He celebrated who they were becoming and reminded them to "sip slow" as they moved through life, enjoying the process of growth throughout their "wild and precious life." (He liked to quote Mary Oliver.)

Educators who are turtles help kids push their own idea up and out. They come alongside a fundraiser, a project that might not work, or a new venture. The kids generate the ideas, and after giving the kids guidance, the educators give them the credit and celebrate their work.

When we support kids in doing hard things and struggling well, we help them gain the experience they need for gritty optimism. Their hope for the future will be based in evidence that new possibilities are within their reach. This is all part of welcoming kids into a world of responsibility *and* joy.

Another part of it, which we'll explore next, is pointing them to reliable sources of truth. Can TikTok answer life's questions?

TAKEAWAY

Doing hard things with others can lead to joy and develops a gritty optimism based on evidence and experience. The best way to do hard things is with others.

TRY THIS

Think of one to three kids you know. What are their talents? Write them down for each kid.

Sometime this week, look each kid in the eye and tell them about the talents you see.

Also, ask them:

- What is something you can do now with that talent that seemed hard last year?
- What is something you would like to be able to do a year from now that seems really hard now?
- What steps would you need to take to get there?
- How can I help?

6
TIKTOK IS NOT TRUTH

A few years ago, my family and I climbed the Sydney Harbour Bridge in Australia, which stands 440 feet above the harbor and provides an incredible view of the iconic Sydney Opera House. Because Australians are less litigious than people in other countries, they let people climb to the top—as long as they are strapped into a safety harness the entire climb. While the Australians are less likely to bring lawsuits, they also understand the truth of gravity.

It does not matter if I believe, you believe, or anyone else believes in gravity. The fact is, if I were to climb that bridge in Sydney without a harness and then jump, I would either plunge into the harbor or create a mess on the road below. As novelist Flannery O'Connor once wrote, "The truth does not change according to our ability to stomach it."[1]

There are some things in life that are fundamentally true, like gravity, and then there are things that are unclear, subjective, and debatable, like a large percentage of what you might find on TikTok. Increasingly, our society is confusing these two categories.

Curiosity can serve as a bridge between them. We live in a world that is becoming less curious and more certain that anyone who disagrees with us is an enemy. But I don't believe we are enemies if we have different beliefs.

For instance, maybe my assertion that there are things that are fundamentally true offends you. If it does, I wonder why. Does this claim sound oppressive? Do you have beliefs that you think are true? I think we all do. Is one element of truth for you that nothing is fundamentally true? If that is the case, that makes me genuinely curious about you, because our perspectives inform our understanding of truth and provide purpose—an essential element of curiosity that cultivates joy.

Discerning truth in a virtual world with algorithms that monetize our attention and pit people against one another is increasingly difficult. Often the content is deliberately deceptive—the more outrageous, the better—in order to increase the likelihood of viral spread.

A quick Google search of "outrageous TikTok truth claim examples" returned these remarkable "truths":

- A "doomsday eclipse" will cause the world to go dark for six minutes on August 2, 2025.
- Garlic can prevent COVID-19.
- 5G causes cancer.
- The Earth is hollow and contains an inner world.

We all can breathe a big sigh of relief after surviving the August 2025 doomsday eclipse!

How many ridiculous arguments have we witnessed in TikTok comments? How many snarky debates have we engaged in? These posts are designed to get a rise out of us, not to communicate things that are incontrovertibly true.

Yet more people are turning to TikTok as a news source. In 2020, 3 percent of U.S. adults regularly got their news on the app, and that number grew to 17 percent in 2024. For eighteen-to-twenty-nine-year-olds, the growth over those four years was from 9 to 39 percent.[2] Nearly half of young adults are getting their "news" from TikTok, which uses an algorithm to keep their attention without any particular regard for truth. This is bad news on multiple levels, as short-form videos (SFV) of the sort on TikTok, Instagram Reels, and YouTube Shorts seem to be eroding truth and attention. A recent analysis of seventy-one studies with almost one hundred thousand participants found that increased viewing of SFVs was related to reduced cognition, attention, and inhibitory control, as well as increased stress and anxiety.[3] While cause and effect are difficult to establish without more research, these findings are probably not shocking to any of us who have lost ourselves in reel after reel.

Society's relationship with claims portrayed as facts goes far beyond social media and the modern era. Humans have been victims of propaganda for years and across cultures, the most well-known of which occurred in Nazi Germany. Many in the United States have perpetuated hateful, baseless information over the years that supported deplorable actions: slavery, Jim Crow, segregation, and reservations for Native Americans, to name a few. Sadly, the list of examples extends well into the present and will extend into the future.

The past demonstrates that social media is not the cause of our misunderstanding of truth; the people of previous generations did not need social media to convince them of objectively false information that destroyed lives, cultures, and trust in institutions. Social media is only an accelerant for this kind of destruction.

Kids are looking for answers on TikTok, but we can invite them into a far better experience. In this chapter, we will unpack how fostering curiosity and productively struggling to uncover truth—probably not on SFVs—can cultivate joy.

Let's start with this question: Why are humans so susceptible to false information of the type we often see on social media?

TRUTH, CERTAINTY, AND CURIOSITY

With so much uncertainty in the world, we long for certainty. We want explanations for mysteries. We are attracted to echoes of our own inferences, tending to favor information that aligns with our present assumptions, which leads to confirmation bias.

There is a mix of healthy and unhealthy components here: Curiosity drives us to gain more understanding and is critical for growth. But being blinded by our biases can rob us of discovery, and a desire for simplistic certainty can crush critical thinking and make us gullible. In fact, one study found that people most likely to deny scientific consensus were not misinformed; they believed they were the best informed and were the least likely to change their minds.[4]

I believe the ultimate reason we're attracted to claims that sound certain is that humans simply are wired to search for truth. Truth is actually the source of both curiosity and certainty. In a world filled with truth, there is always more to be discovered. We look for it everywhere—even, as J. R. R. Tolkien once said, in the world of fantasy.

The author of the Lord of the Rings trilogy, which has sold over 150 million copies, believed that fantasy stories endure because people are drawn to the deeper narratives within them. He asserted that humans have an intuition that an underlying reality exists that is universally true and leads to joy.

Tolkien put it this way: "The peculiar quality of the 'joy' in successful Fantasy can thus be explained by a sudden glimpse of the underlying reality or truth."[5]

Not a sudden glimpse of a wild claim you might see on social media.

Instead, a glimpse of something that humans, over centuries, have found to be undeniably true. What are some of these realities?

We want good to triumph over evil. We want to escape death. We want a perfect love from which we will not part. As Tolkien wrote, "We want joy beyond the walls of the world, poignant as grief."[6] And as reliable as the law of gravity, evil brings darkness, and goodness brings light. Cruelty harms, and love heals.

There are many more undeniable realities of the world and the human experience. Do we ever get to a point in life where we know them all? No. Because of our finite nature, no amount of human learning or maturity would result in full awareness and mastery.

Xiaodong Lin is a Columbia University professor who has studied Nobel Prize winners, and he discovered a key commonality among them: "They all have insatiable passion and hunger to discover the truth about a problem. Winning a Nobel Prize was never these people's motive for their hard work."[7] A desire for truth feeds an "insatiable passion" that is about discovery, not success.

Are we ever meant to have our curiosity diminished?

If Nobel Prize winners would answer no, it is an easy bet that you and I should respond with a resounding no as well.

We adults have much to offer young people, but we do not know everything. As hard as it may be for us to admit it, we have areas of ignorance. In a world filled with truth, and as humans who are wired for truth-seeking, we can gain a great deal more from curiosity than we can from some false certainty that we already know all we need to know. In a world where we turn anyone who disagrees with us into an enemy, curiosity is the antidote.

When adults model and teach curiosity about undeniable truths in life, a few things happen:

- Both adults and kids discover deeper truth through others' perspectives.
- We create an environment for respectful dialogue.
- We can engage in productive struggle grounded in truth within loving community, which leads to joy.

ADULT CURIOSITY ABOUT KIDS' PERSPECTIVES

Curious people are driven by the belief that there is truth to be known about others' lived experiences. Curiosity is what drove me and thirteen school administrators to each shadow a student for an entire day.

At 7:15 a.m., I met Ashley Castro, a seventeen-year-old junior in high school, in the cafeteria. She seemed a bit shy—not surprising, as I am a random professor from Texas who is sixteen inches taller than her. The bell rang, and 2,200 students promptly began choreographed movements up and down multiple staircases.

"Stay close—the stairways can be a little crazy," Ashley warned as we made our way to her first-period art class. After she skillfully guided me through the hallways, we entered her classroom, and she set a stool next to hers for me to use.

My kids give me a hard time for asking people so many questions, but I always am curious to know other people's stories—especially kids' stories. Throughout this art class, Ashley shared some of hers.

"Before school, what does your morning look like?" I asked.

"I have to get my ten- and thirteen-year-old brother and sister ready by seven o'clock," Ashley explained. "My mom works third shift in a plastics factory about thirty minutes away and gets home right at seven, so we have to get ready on our own if we are going to get to school on time."

I asked many other questions, including, "Do you work in addition to school?"

"I work at two different restaurants mostly on the weekends, but sometimes I pick up some shifts during the week," Ashley answered. "On Sundays, I work at one restaurant from eight to three o'clock, and then at the other one from four to nine o'clock."

Even with the external burdens she was carrying, she could not wait for me to get to her social studies class.

"Why? Do you love social studies?" I asked.

"No. I used to hate it. But Ms. Rios makes it seem like it matters to us. We research why things are the way they are and how we can change them. Also, she cares about us. If I have beef with my friends, she will talk with us about it."

Ms. Rios did not disappoint. At the front of her room, there was a handmade poster that read, "I bug you 'cause I love you." She spent the first five minutes of class celebrating the growth students recently had shown on college admissions tests. Ms. Rios gave one student who demonstrated the most growth on the test a stuffed lion (the school's mascot) to have on her desk for the rest of the class period. I watched a seventeen-year-old girl who looked like a full-grown woman beam proudly over being designated the "lion of the day."

Next, Ashley navigated us through the socially complex world of lunch. She expertly helped me select the best entrée that day—a turkey sandwich with the right chips—then weaved through traffic to get me a bottle of water. We sat down with a table of Latinas, and I spent thirty minutes getting a glimpse of the world through their eyes.

They told me about an art show at the school that night, and

Ashley invited me to see her drawing that would be displayed. When I accepted her offer, I got to appreciate up close a carefully drawn depiction of Ashley's own eye—a good reminder of how we need to seek truth through the eyes of others.

In addition to the little glimpse of her life I had through that school day, I was able to experience her generous hospitality and genuine curiosity about me and my work.

Could I have gotten the same knowledge through a TikTok reel of Ashley? No. The truth of her life that I understood after spending the day with her was so much richer and more rewarding than curated social-media content. I did not just get to learn *about her* through a virtual filter. I got to know *her* as a person.

A few weeks after my visit, two of her administrators arrived on Baylor's campus for a master's class I was teaching, and they brought me something from Ashley. In return for a couple of Baylor T-shirts and a note I had given to her, she had sent me her eye drawing in a frame.

Ashley's drawing now hangs on my office wall beside my diplomas, reminding me that we might learn more about truth from our kids than we do from degree programs. The deeper truth of a human who has lived such a different experience from my own is the peak of understanding[8]—it is empathy.[9]

EMPATHY THAT SUPPORTS TRUTH-SEEKING

For those of us who are pouring into the next generation, empathy means seeing things through their eyes. If you are a parent, is there a picture book you read hundreds of times with your kids when they were little? In our family, that book was *No, David!*, a story about a boy who repeatedly gets in trouble. Every time we turned to the page with David picking his nose or running down the street with his backside exposed, our kids would belly-laugh. The book was a joy to read over and over when my wife or I saw the story from their perspective.

As a science teacher, I taught science concepts with labs and demonstrations that I had performed dozens of times. I knew what would happen when the dry ice sublimated, or the rockets ignited, or when I lit the alcohol-soaked hundred-dollar bill on fire. I loved those labs, not because of my own scientific discovery, but because it was the students' first time seeing those demonstrations, and it helped them break through to understanding. As a coach, I have run the same layup drills in basketball practices countless times, but the joy came when a player who had been struggling with an off-hand layup finally figured it out.

If we are parenting, teaching, or coaching exclusively from our perspective, then we miss the magic that comes when we discover others' experiences. We will miss the spark in a child's imagination while reading a book, the realization of why a basketball player is jumping off the inside foot when taking a layup, or the light-bulb moment of a budding scientist grasping how the world around her works. When we witness these moments, we experience their joy as they discover truth that can launch them into becoming more of who they are meant to be.

The key to entering into these moments? Curiosity. If we are going to support kids in their pursuit of truth, we must see the world through their eyes.[10]

We think we know what it is like to be a kid and a student because, with varying degrees of success or frustration, we have been in these roles. But when was the last time we were kids and students? The world has changed fundamentally since I was a kid and student, but truth has not. So, as we support young people in truth-seeking, we get to deepen our own understanding of truth—because seeing from their perspective as we seek truth together develops empathy.[11]

DISCOVERY IN LOVING COMMUNITY

Every summer at Baylor University, I speak to more than five thousand students and parents, welcoming them to what I consider to be one of the most joyful college campuses in the world. Why do I say this? Because I see us pursuing joy through truth and love. I get to invite those young people into four years of productive struggle grounded in truth and loving community.

Each student brings his or her own experiences and perspectives to class, and we can hold those experiences up against truth. Student experiences are what make classes that I have taught for years infinitely interesting.

Since its inception, the primary purpose of a university is to pursue truth through teaching and research.[12] Many universities still do this well in the natural sciences, physical sciences, engineering, and medical schools. Some have lost their way in the humanities and social sciences, where truth has become relative, which contradicts the very nature of truth. Some will say no one can make assertions of what truth is, because their claims will be subjective to their race, gender, culture, and level of privilege.

One of the most frustrating conversations I have ever had with a social science faculty member was about the purpose of research. When I referred to the purpose of research as a pursuit of truth, he responded, "All truth is relative. You cannot assert your truth as a white, heterosexual man, because your truth is based on your privilege."

A bit exasperated with my fellow white, heterosexual, male colleague, I asked, "Then what would you say is the point of research?"

"Research is just advocacy of a particular position," he answered. Essentially, he was saying that researchers do not interrogate truth in a loving community; they are simply attempting to convince others that they are "more right" than someone else.

But without truth—durable, fundamental truth—how would we even determine who is "more right"?

Research as advocacy has no regard for discovering fundamental truths or listening to a loving community. Seems a little like TikTok claims and debates, doesn't it?

If we do not accept that undeniable, universal truth exists, how can we deepen our understanding of it? How can we even grasp it if it is entirely subjective, with claims of "my truth, your truth, or their truth"?

The good news is that fundamental truths are durable and become richer and deeper through interrogation.

Higher education should be the very place where ideas are tested to determine what is fundamentally true and what might hold some truth. In my leadership classes, students read a wide array of authors who disagree about the causes and cures for societal ills, because cognitive dissonance primes brains for learning. By having students examine varying viewpoints, we create space for learning. After establishing parameters for our discussion, we try to bring every perspective represented in the classroom into the conversation, since others' lived experiences can reveal the complexity of issues we might oversimplify due to ignorance.

In short, my students struggle with varying ideas, claims, and perspectives so they can get to truth. The best way to do that is in a loving community that values others even when they disagree. The goal is not liberal progress or conservative orthodoxy.[13] The goal is joy that arrives through truth and love.

Earlier in this book, we discussed how joy emerges through struggle. In chapter 2 we saw how Harvard researchers have asserted that a good life comes from "precisely the things that make it hard." This means we have to reconcile truth with struggle; it will not just drop into our lap from a TikTok post. We have to be willing to let go of the comfort of certainty enough to be curious to struggle productively in loving community, so we can discover something new—about the world, others, or even ourselves.

DIFFERENT VERSIONS OF TRUTH?

Unfortunately, much of higher education has become a hostile environment for dialogue that values and explores varying perspectives on key issues. Discussions on sex, gender, identity, politics, the environment, or families can become opportunities to silence those who do not agree with the loudest voices, typically declaring that anyone who disagrees is "intolerant."

But silencing the views of someone with whom we disagree does not allow for struggle that can lead us to truth. Neither does accepting that everyone has a different version of truth—which is a common yet destabilizing concept in the culture forming young people today.

In his book *Selfless*, Stanford professor Brian Lowery asserted that there is no internalized self. "Selves don't emanate from some ineffable light within people. Instead, selves are . . . constructed and reconstructed in a swirl of ever-evolving relationships," he wrote.[14]

Based on this type of thinking, we are simply what we can get others to believe about us.

Lowery supported his point with the 2015 case of Rachel Dolezal, who identified as a Black woman and served as the president of a National Association for the Advancement of Colored People (NAACP) chapter. When it was discovered that both of her biological parents were white, a national uproar ensued. People were deeply offended that someone would claim to be Black when, genetically, that was not the case. Lowery pushed back on this public furor, contending that if Dolezal believed she was Black and others believed she was Black, then she was Black.

Ibram X. Kendi also has made a case that race is socially constructed, highlighting that the term *race* did not exist until the fourteenth-century Portuguese slave trade used it to justify enslaving people who were a different color.[15]

Contrast this discussion with the pervasive view in higher education that gender is fluid. In my leadership capstone class for undergraduate students at Baylor, we wrestle with this question: Why does most of Gen Z accept gender fluidity and not racial fluidity?

I highlight the complexity of the question by noting that experts view both race and gender as socially constructed, but they consider sex as something "assigned at birth." Almost all of us have an XX or an XY chromosome in every cell, which traditionally has dictated whether we are male or female. While society has made room for a wide range of socially constructed genders, many people do not make the same allowance for race—which is odd because 99.9 percent of human DNA across races is similar.[16]

So, if race is socially constructed, as Lowery and Kendi have suggested, and gender also is socially constructed, as sociologists and anthropologists have told us, then why is one acceptable to be fluid and the other is not?

For most of Gen Z, if a white man identifies as a woman, that is not a problem. But if a white woman identifies as a Black woman, that is a huge problem. This is the nonsensical world in which our kids are growing up.

Imagine being a middle schooler living in Lowery's world. You are what you can get others to believe about you. One day, you are a great athlete, student, friend, and male who is about to reach puberty, and you might be interested in girls. The next, you are a terrible athlete after you lose the basketball game for your team, a bad student who failed a test, a terrible friend based on a viral social-media post, and maybe you are not a male because you haven't hit puberty yet.

Having a self that is constantly "constructed and reconstructed in a swirl of ever-evolving relationships" sounds confusing—and possibly despairing, if you don't yet know that your human value is not determined by your performance or by others' views of you. The whiplash this creates cannot lead young people to joy because it is not true.

The truth is that the kid in the previous paragraph did lose the game and fail the test. He might have been a bad friend and hasn't yet hit puberty. Those things can all be true, and there can still be joy. When kids do not see their value as performance-contingent, they can recognize that others' opinions do not define them. Grounding their self-worth in the truth that each human has intrinsic value will give them security and resilience as they grow up.

Possibly our most important role in the lives of the next generation is to ensure that they are seen and known through the lens of truth and deeply loved because they are human. No additional requirements needed.

That does not, however, mean that anything goes. We love kids well when we tell them the truth about who they are.

RESILIENT TRUTH

We have touched on some controversial areas in this chapter, and I am curious if you disagree, and, if so, why.

When I brought up Lowery and Kendi, two progressive Black academics, I wonder what your reaction was. Were you encouraged because you had been concerned about the positions I hold as a white, heterosexual male up until this point in the book? If you were uncomfortable, was it because you feared I might be a liberal snowflake who assigns readings from authors like these?

However we might disagree, would you be curious about why I came to the perspectives I have and be willing to share your perspectives with me? Could we have a respectful exchange of ideas without turning the other into an enemy?

With enough curiosity and practice, I think we could.

We may be lacking in those areas if we primarily try to discern truth on social media—which, again, monetizes our attention by pitting our views against each other, rewards viral attention grabs and unnuanced claims, and turns users into products that are sold to advertisers. The same thing can happen when we seek truth in a community that lacks diversity of thought, which provides no opportunities to struggle respectfully with the perspectives of others.

As I mentioned previously, I read a wide range of perspectives with my students to help us better understand truth. I do the same thing with my own kids. I intentionally invite them to struggle, and I try to support them as they do.

How could this look for you and the young people in your life?

Here is the great thing about truth: it is resilient. You can hold any perspective up to it without fear. So go ahead and pressure-test it. Interrogate it. Even get angry with it. Truth is not fragile, and our evolving perception of it cannot change it—just like we can't change gravity. It is an underlying reality of the world that we, along with the young people around us, can discover more about through curiosity. Certainty saps curiosity of its power and can slow our pursuit of truth.

In the coming pages, we'll explore why we tend to confine ourselves to echo chambers and why we grow the most when we engage with a vibrant world filled with people who are not like us.

Sound uncomfortable?

Sure—but that's okay. We know by now that hard things can lead to joy.

TAKEAWAY

Curiosity is better than certainty because curiosity leads to truth that can fuel joy.

TRY THIS

As adults who are interested in pursuing truth, we need to read divergent views and welcome perspectives from all backgrounds because that enriches conversations. Find different authors, influences, or friends who have very different perspectives.

With young people present, start a conversation in which you only ask questions that seek to better understand their positions. Resist the urge to be certain about what you think you know about their positions. Just be curious. Almost any holiday gathering could be a good venue to try this out!

If you do not want to do this in person, read or watch different thought leaders' perspectives and discuss them with kids.

Two goals of this conversation: (1) that each perspective would be heard to better understand truth and (2) that kids would see the joy that comes from curiosity about others.

7
ECHO CHAMBERS BREED INSECURITY

Do you ever feel like we adults are still living in middle school?

There may be fewer awkward moments involving braces, pimples, and voice changes, but we have not quite shaken the cafeteria clique culture, have we? While we might not have to pick our lunch table groups anymore, we still find some of our identity in the groups with which we choose to associate.

Sometimes we go so far as to identify with a group and then determine what we believe, even when we might think it is the other way around.[1]

For example, what do you believe about people in these categories?

- Democrat versus Republican
- actor versus veteran
- thirty-five-year-old versus seventy-five-year-old
- union leader versus executive

We can make a lot of assumptions about groups on the left and groups on the right, feeling confident we know what they are for and against. We might even think we know who they are.

Need proof? What images pop into your mind when you read this phrase: "Republican veteran who is a seventy-five-year-old executive"?

What do you see when you read this one: "Democrat actor who is a thirty-five-year-old union leader"?

Pick the one who is least like you and consider: Do you want to spend time with him? Would he tolerate you? If he would tolerate you, would he also celebrate you? Would you vilify or mock him? Would you want to learn from him?

If you would have little openness to this kind of interaction and no curiosity about a person unlike you, it is worth exploring why. Perhaps you think you already know all you need to know about him based on labels.

Is this all that different from scanning the lunchroom for someone to sit with, making quick judgments as you seek similarity and likely acceptance? The hard truth is that the same insecurity driving our behavior in the middle-school cafeteria is still driving us today as we seek and stay in echo chambers.

If we adults are still doing this, how will kids ever see a different way to operate?

We will need to replace our insecurity with confident humility—which will cultivate curiosity—in order to push past uncharitable assumptions about others. In this chapter we will look closer at how we slip into tribal thinking patterns and why echo chambers limit our joy. We will also explore practical ways we can change our priorities and habits, and the good that can come from young people joining us in encountering perspectives far different from their own.

PASSING DOWN INCURIOUS INSECURITY

Earlier I listed contrasting categories of people, such as Democrat and Republican. What if I told you all those characteristics described the same person at different stages of life?

During a visit to this person's home, I found artifacts of a confidently humble life. He lived with his wife in a small adobe home that was over one hundred years old. They slept in two twin beds they had zip-tied together—beds that had been left behind by the previous owner. Along the drive, he had built a fence out of pieces of telephone poles he had gotten a deal on. His garage shelves were lined with peanut butter jars filled with screws, bolts, and nails. The window by the kitchen table where he often worked looked out on a pond with a dock he had built.

He also welcomed Queen Elizabeth II, Mikhail Gorbachev, and other heads of state to this simple 1,800-square-foot house.

This home (and those various characteristics above) belonged to Ronald Reagan.

Regardless of your political persuasion, I hope these facts spark your curiosity about this man—not only because he was the fortieth president of the United States but because anyone around you is deserving of your interest. Sadly, many of us have become uncharitably incurious, and it is a trait that we can pass down to the next generation.

Another behavior we seem to be passing to the next generation is the need to broadcast our opinions to the world as soon as a thought passes through our minds. Just because we have the ability to vilify, condemn, and decry someone else with a worldwide megaphone—creating a permanent record of our spur-of-the-moment rage—why do we think that is what the world needs?

Every public tragedy is an opportunity to demonize the people we disagree with—a time to fire a flare into the virtual cosmos to let our echo chamber know we are unified in our disdain for the "out group." Not only are we not interested in the other side's stories; we want to categorically destroy the story and sometimes the people as well.

We start modeling this behavior for our kids when they are young. What do they hear us say around the dinner table when they listen to us in conflict with someone? How do we talk about politics, culture, or the world?

For me, there have been two checks on my propensity to demean others in front of my kids. First, although not always appreciated by me in the moment, I have a wife who calls me out when I get negative about a teacher, colleague, or family member around our kids. Sometimes it is just a disapproving look. Other times she might say something like, "There might be another side to that story."

Second, there is nothing more conscience-pricking than hearing my own words coming out of my kids' mouths. I noticed this first when I was watching basketball games with my son. As young as five years old, he would complain about officiating and other teams, using what felt like oddly familiar phrasing.

"How is that not a foul?"

"What was the ref looking at? This is ridiculous!"

"I cannot stand those fans. They are so annoying!"

It is safe to say these moments gave me an opportunity for self-reflection and soul-searching.

Kids pick up on our opinions of others, politics, and culture whether we are paying attention or not. They can figure out if we are curious or closed off about others.

We are primary influences on our kids until their peers and

social media start to supplant us. On average, teens spend more than 4.8 hours on social media per day.[2] Social media is designed to be an echo chamber, where both kids and adults get sucked into a world that confirms our opinions, justifies our positions, and keeps our eyes on screens.

Now kids are dealing with the ultimate echo chamber: chatbots. These are AI-generated "companions," "thought partners," or "co-intelligences," like Gemini, Copilot, ChatGPT, and Claude, which scrape large language models to give advice. Even the anthropomorphic names used for the chatbots are disturbing.

Nearly three out of four teens (72 percent) have used a chatbot for companionship.[3] About one-third of teens find AI conversations satisfying or more satisfying than human conversations, and one-third would choose AI over humans for serious conversations.[4]

Further, teens are turning to chatbots for therapy.[5] While there is some possible upside to teens being able to access support that might otherwise be unavailable, many chatbots give feedback that is 50 percent more sycophantic than humans.[6] Its advice often validates and does not challenge the teen's thinking.[7]

Whenever we surround ourselves with voices exactly like our own, whether in the virtual realm or in the physical world, we can easily lose sight of reality. How can we possibly see more than our own tiny vantage point in the broad landscape of life?

When we no longer want to know stories that are different from our own, we lock ourselves in echo chambers and throw away the key. We're convinced we already know all we need to know about the people "over there"—and they do not deserve our time.

How can we expect kids to grow up when we act like adult middle schoolers?

A POLARIZED WORLD OF ANXIETY AND ENEMIES

In Robert Putnam and Shaylyn Romney Garrett's book, *The Upswing: How America Came Together a Century Ago and How We Can Do It Again*, the authors give a description of the United States in the early 1900s that sounds startlingly similar to the modern era:

> In an America transformed by the rapid forward march of technology, new forms of communication and transportation have disconnected and reconnected people in countless ways, rearranging identities, beliefs, and value systems. Some optimistically tout the breaking of barriers and narrowing of distances between people, while many others experience loneliness, isolation, and atomization as traditional social structures give way. . . . Even the reliability of the free press, that critical component of any democratic system, has become questionable, as a drive for profit overpowers a responsibility to check truth.[8]

Echo chambers, distrust, and polarization are not new.

In fact, Putnam and Romney Garrett argue that the United States has moved from "I" to "we" and back to "I" over the last 125 years based on economic, cultural, social, and political data. Following the Civil War, the country was fractured, polarized, and individualistic. Americans found it easy to sit in echo chambers of like-minded people, becoming increasingly entrenched in their positions around race, voting rights, religion, and lightly regulated capitalism, to name a few wedge issues.

At the turn of the century, there was a movement away from "I" to "we" as a society. Nearly all U.S. civic membership organizations (e.g., Elks, Rotary, Kiwanis, NAACP, PTA, Boy Scouts, Girl Scouts) that, at their peak, enrolled more than 1 percent of the population were founded between 1870 and 1920.[9] As a country, people became more convinced that we were all in this together. This spirit remained steadfast through the Depression, World War II, and the following two decades.

In the 1960s, there was a move toward individualism for a variety of reasons. For the purposes of our discussion, that movement has only continued and even accelerated since the 1960s. Although one of the most popular songs of the 2006 phenomenon *High School Musical* was "We're All in This Together," that has not been Gen Z's experience.

Let's hope that moving beyond a polarized world filled with anxiety will not require another Great Depression or world war. The good news is that Putnam and Romney Garrett found that the move toward "we" started well before World War I or the 1929 stock market crash.

As adults, we will need to model and teach how to move beyond just listening to people we identify with and start moving toward the stories of people who are different from us. In a culture that demonizes those with whom we disagree, we need to become curious about the stories that led them to different perspectives—curiosity fed by humility.

FROM ARROGANT INSECURITY TO CONFIDENT HUMILITY

At its core, arrogance is incurious. Arrogant people do not need to understand anyone else's perspectives. Why would they need to understand others when they already understand everything?

An underlying quality feeding that arrogance is insecurity. When we as humans feel that things are out of control, we grasp for control, and researchers have found that the less we know, the more certain we are about what we think we know.[10] This is true about factual information *and* the way we interact with others.

For most of us, when we feel insecure in an environment, we cling to what we know. In middle school, that meant having the same opinion as the cool kids with status, wearing the same clothes, or making fun of the kids with less status. When we step into new or unstable environments as adults, we revert to tribal behavior, looking for anyone who might seem like us or share a similar perspective. Just watch what happens when people walk into an opposing team's stadium, start a new job, or attend a party where they know only a few people. When we feel insecure, we seek security in similarity.

When we already feel secure, however, we don't need to seek similarity and are free to be curious. We can move outside of our own myopic perspectives because we are not focused on ourselves. A black-and-white world of self-focus opens up to a Technicolor world filled with others. As concern for ourselves decreases, focus on others can increase.

Think of the rare kids in middle school who seemed to float between cliques and lunch tables, making others feel like they mattered. As adults, these are the people we do not always notice because when we interact with them, we walk away feeling better about ourselves. They made us feel like we were the most interesting people in the room.

Curiosity by its very nature is humble. It puts us in the vulnerable position of admitting that we do not know things—how things work, how others feel, why others feel certain ways, why we exist. It is hard to be vulnerable with others when we do not feel secure. Humility requires confidence that we are secure, we have intrinsic value, and others do as well.

When we can move away from insecurity expressed as arrogance, we can develop confidence that comes from humility and approach all kinds of people with curiosity.[11]

DO WE HAVE THE STORY?

As a new student in Highlands Ranch, Colorado, Keonte[12] had transferred from a Denver public school. His mom felt his previous school was not challenging him appropriately, so she brought him to the private school where Tige Watson was the director of student affairs.

Keonte was not sure he wanted to stay. He was uncomfortable in his new environment and, among other things, missed his friends from his old school. It wasn't long before Tige found him crying in the counselor's office. Tige assured Keonte that being successful at the private school was well within his abilities.

Keonte returned the next day, committed to trying his best. He progressed from standing outside the STEM room and peering through the windows to becoming an active part of the robotics class.

A recurring issue began to emerge, though—dress-code violations. Keonte was getting dress-coded daily for sagging pants, and Tige began hearing about it from his staff. Teachers said Keonte must be "trying to act gangster."

One even said, "I don't know why he's here."

A few days later, Tige saw Keonte sitting in the hall and approached him.

"Stand up," Tige told him.

When Keonte stood, his pants were sagging well below his waist.

"You cannot sag your pants here, Keonte. I need you to pull them up."

"I can't," was his reply.

"Why?"

"I can't," Keonte repeated.

As Tige began to respond, Keonte finally pulled his pants up, revealing that they were about six inches too short. Tige could see his socks and ankles.

Keonte began to cry. "I can't because I don't have pants long enough. These are the only pants I have."

"I am so sorry, Keonte," Tige replied quickly. "Let them sag. Tell anyone who asks to come talk to me."

That evening, Tige went to his own closet, took out his six pairs of jeans, and put them in a bag. The next day, he brought them to school and looked for Keonte in the hall.

As soon as they made eye contact, Keonte sheepishly pulled his pants up, thinking he might get reprimanded again. Instead, Tige brought him to his office and handed him the bag.

Keonte's face lit up. "Is this for me?"

"They are all yours."

"I'm going to put a pair on right now," Keonte said and quickly changed.

He asked Tige if he would keep the bag in his office until the end of the school day, to make sure no one took it from him. Then he hugged Tige and left for class.

When Tige shared what he had learned with his staff, two were visibly emotional. "Do we have the story?" became a sort of mantra for their staff.

Do we have the story? That would be a good mantra for all of us.

What would it look like if you and the young people around you paused and explored that question more often?

"STORYSEEKING" MOVES US AWAY FROM ECHO CHAMBERS

Life is so much richer when we are surrounded by others' stories. If kids are going to grow in confidence that allows them to humbly seek out and learn from others, they need to become great "storyseekers." Yes, *storyseeking* is a made-up word, but it is one we need to become familiar with if we want to help our kids grow up.

Hearing others' stories helps young people think in possibilities, not probabilities. It can normalize struggle, enhance a sense of belonging, and help them identify purpose beyond themselves. Angus Fletcher, professor of story science through Project Narrative at Ohio State University, argues that humans have a narrative intelligence that allows us to use stories as cognitive tools that build resilience and spread joy.[13]

Hearing from a great athlete, a parent, a friend, or even a new acquaintance that everyone goes through hard things—and that hard things can lead to joy—increases the likelihood that kids will persevere.[14] It also will help them to become great storyseekers.

How can we help young people seek out stories? By modeling it ourselves.

I am proud to admit that I have lived almost my entire life in "flyover country." My people are not coastal elites who look down on the good people who feed the world, look out for their neighbors, and think college football and basketball are the pinnacles of entertainment. As power coalesces around a few key spots, like Silicon Valley, New York City, and Washington, DC, assumptions about "undesirable" places and people can filter down to kids, especially if they are seeking influence.

What you think of rural communities in West Virginia, South Carolina, and Mississippi likely depends on where you are from. Your assumptions probably will be significantly different if you grew up in Manhattan, Kansas, rather than Manhattan, New York.

If there is anything that my many years in school have taught me, it is that kids are kids wherever you go, but different contexts affect their opportunities to flourish. You could even say that I am a natural experiment in how context affects flourishing.

My family moved to the coalfields of West Virginia when I was sixteen years old, after my dad had to find a new job. Our new town had a welcome sign made from a chain-link fence, and we lived on Rural Route 2 up Lick Creek Holler. A holler is a narrow valley, and ours was near Booger Hole Holler and Slippery Gut Holler. Suffice it to say, those two years of high school taught me what it was like to not have a lot of opportunities. That community, however, was also the reason for one life-altering opportunity.

Fortunately for me at the time, because I looked like Appalachian poverty, the federal government offered me a college scholarship that I did not have to pay back as long as I taught for six years after graduation. I would not have had that opportunity if I had not graduated from a rural West Virginia high school.

For the past five years, I have spent a week in March driving all over rural South Carolina through small towns like Bishopville, Hanahan, and Rembert. With tremendous appreciation for Waze and bursts of magenta azaleas along country roads, I have made my way through one small town speed trap after another, so I can learn from these rural communities that are trying to recruit and retain teachers.

I also work in Mississippi in communities like Tishomingo, Chalybeate, and Pontotoc, where we are working with schools to reduce opioid use by building thriving learning communities.

One of the greatest personal benefits of spending time in these places is being reminded that life is so much richer when we get to know others' stories. Spend some time talking to a parent or teacher at the Chat N' Chew or Nick's BBQ and Drive-In, and I guarantee, you will be shaken out of your echo chamber in life-giving ways.

Parents everywhere desire what is best for their kids, have hopes and dreams, and want their kids to have more opportunities than they did. Not all these people look like you, but you likely have more in common with them than you think.

And when you identify differences, allow them to be there. Their perspective doesn't have to threaten yours. Accept who they are with respect, allowing them to broaden your world, knowing that others' stories are an antidote to ignorance.

So get off social media and go for a drive with your kid. Stop by a diner and see who you meet and have a conversation! I promise it will be more beneficial than a reel that mocks a boomer, a post that vilifies a rival, or a comment that dehumanizes someone else.

The key for us and our kids is to get more comfortable with being uncomfortable. Vulnerability is uncomfortable, *and* we get far more comfortable with this when we grow in confident humility. Tige did not immediately have the answers for how best to support Keonte. I did not want to move to West Virginia as a teenager—a place I had no answers for. I was entering a closed society that saw me as an outsider. In my insecurity, I am sure I came across as arrogant at times. Humble confidence would have made me more curious. As an adult, I do not know the lives of people in rural South Carolina whose communities have declined due to the loss of industry. I certainly do not have all the answers for reducing opioid use in Mississippi. Humble confidence is what gives me the ability to know that there are answers for how to grow thriving learning communities in these areas—but those answers are contextual. One of the best gifts we can give our kids is being curious about others' stories.

The greatest blessing of meeting new people is that it gets a lot harder to "other" them when we actually get to know them in their context. For us and our kids, seeking others' stories is far better than focusing more on ourselves.

In the next chapter, we explore how to help kids tell their own stories of breakthrough and understanding. Those stories are the ones that lead to joy.

TAKEAWAY

Echo chambers reinforce arrogant insecurity. Confident humility cultivates knowing and being known. Move out of adult middle school with curiosity fueled by humble confidence.

TRY THIS

The most important question for getting out of your echo chamber is: Who are you most curious about? Are they people who agree or disagree with you? This says a lot about who we are. Move toward people who are not like you.

Ask a couple of kids to tell you something that happened to them before they turned nine that has had the biggest impact on who they have become. If they have trouble coming up with something, start by answering the question yourself. Your vulnerability might unlock a story for them.

If you do not want to go that deep, just have them explain something to you about kids their age that you do not understand (e.g., Why was "6-7" ever funny? If you get the answer, let me know!).

8

HELP KIDS OWN THEIR STORIES

College exams are always a challenge, but as professors, we hope they do not cause students to spiral. Sadly, that is exactly what happened for one college student when she had a panic attack during an exam.

Later, when she met with a therapist about it, the therapist asked her to describe in detail what had happened.

The student said she became "flushed, and lightheaded"; her heart "was pounding, and her hands felt clammy." She felt like running out of the room—but she did not leave. She took the test and "did okay."

The gripping fear of another panic attack, however, was keeping her from attempting a second test.

The therapist tried to help the student positively reframe the first test as an example of perseverance through anxiety, but the student was resistant. She persisted in telling herself a story of anxiety that was keeping her from functioning adequately.

"Yes, but I had a panic attack," was her habitual reply to the therapist.[1]

For the student, the story was all about the panic attack and her deficiencies. Even though perseverance was evident in her story, she would not focus on anything positive and found herself in a vicious cycle of paralyzing inadequacy.

She needed to understand how she overcame the panic attack and own the fact that she persevered. Only then would she release her sense of unworthiness and enter a world where she was capable of becoming more.

Can you think of a young person in your life who has a similar story? Maybe you have one yourself.

All of us need to identify stories from our lives when we were surprised by what we were able to do. This is especially true for kids. It is great to tell kids stories of times when we surprised ourselves or where we have seen others persevere, but when kids find their own stories of prior perseverance, they begin to change.[2] If they get the story wrong, they do not change.

We have to help kids seek their own stories, because those stories will become their source of resilience, curiosity, and eventually joy.

Young people need to tell their own stories of overcoming adversity, especially when they were surprised by how they did it. As they tell themselves these stories, they begin to imagine futures where they and the world around them can become more of what they were meant to be.

The first thing to do as we guide them in this is to make sure the stories they are telling themselves are not lies.

STORIES THAT ARE LIES

I found a crumpled piece of paper from my youngest daughter that humbled and crushed me simultaneously. Grace[3] has always been a free spirit who wanted to stomp in every puddle, save every animal, and attempt any adventure. She is athletic, artistic, beautiful, brilliant, compassionate, and creative. As a family friend once told me, she "moves through the world differently." That is what was so troubling about the crumpled paper.

She had written one accusation after another about herself: "You are: spoiled, entitled, rude, insecure, inconsiderate, ugly, untrustworthy, miserable to be around . . . a disappointment to: your parents, your friends, your siblings, your teachers, and most of all YOURSELF."

How could such an amazing kid—*my* kid—believe those lies about herself? What had fed this kind of crushing narrative? How had I not done a better job combating those lies and helping her find her true story?

Finding this note was a low point for me as a parent. Humble confidence is the only thing that allows me—or, even more importantly, Grace—to share this story. My arrogant insecurity did not want to include it. But if we are going to seek others' stories—the stories that shape and humble us—we have to be vulnerable. At my worst, I am judgmental, so I fear being judged. If you are like me, then that judgment will crush your curiosity about others and your willingness to share.

Grace and I have had many conversations since I found that note, and I have learned so much from her. She is now a talented, confident, and kind kid who is ready to launch into college and the adventures she has always sought. Grace is always the kid who wants to travel with me for work. These trips have allowed her to surf without a wet suit for hours in fifty-four-degree water in New Zealand, hike in the Australian bush, and meet many fascinating people. She dreams of being a nurse, painting, and living on the beach with a golden retriever. As we all do, she still struggles with self-doubt and not finding her identity in her performance, but she is growing in humble confidence.

Humble confidence that leans into her own story does not come naturally to Grace. She is an introvert who needs time to herself to draw, paint, and create. She is not isolating herself through her art. She is connecting to creation and others, as she gives most of her finished work away. Grace found a bigger, richer life by learning from kids and families in the Dominican Republic, experiencing other cultures, and talking through life with others. In fact, getting outside of herself has always been the path to greater joy. Isn't this true for most of us?

HELPING KIDS TELL THEIR TRUE STORIES

Here are four ways we can draw out stories that breathe life into young people.[4]

First, as adults, we must be vulnerable. Sometimes our stories can be catalysts for kids to share their own because they see our vulnerability first and recognize it is okay for them to share. For example, when I share that I dealt with dyslexia as a kid, both kids and adults are more likely to share how they have struggled. We all know that we connect more with others' weaknesses than with their strengths, so this first step of shared weakness always feels vulnerable. The vulnerability continues as we ask questions and listen. Sometimes that means absorbing criticism, carrying others through their pain, or allowing ourselves to enter a space filled with suffering.

For years, I have tried to engineer discomfort out of vulnerability,[5] but based on experience, I now know that is not possible. Maintaining hope in the face of adversity requires a dogged determination to live life for and with others, which means we will experience pain, rejection, and failure on the way to deeper joy.

Second, we need to be curious, listen for what we do not understand, and be sensitive to generational divides. An easy thing to do is to ask kids questions that help us understand those generational divides: "What do you do on social media?" "What do you like about that song or video?" "Why do you believe that?" "What does my generation get wrong about kids?" "How do you react when someone disagrees with you?" Obviously, some of these questions depend on the age of the kid we are asking, but the point is to ask and then just listen. When we open our mouths again, the next thing out of it should be another question that builds on curiosity.

If you are struggling to come up with questions for kids you are genuinely curious about, here are a few of my favorites. I have asked these questions of complete strangers and my own kids, and the questions have been excellent portals into others' stories.

"What was the low point of your life? Turning point? High point?"[6]

I was in another country talking to four strangers, and I used these questions. Within minutes, one person shared, "My low point was my dad dying when I was seven. My turning point was coming to grips with my anger at God when I was sixteen." This response led another person to share about the loss of a parent at a young age. We ran out of time before the two other people could share. Not everyone has to answer every question—I can answer only two of the three questions myself. Far from trauma bonding, these conversations create human connections where we can see and be seen, hear and be heard.

If those questions go too deep too fast for you, another great set is "What was your first, last, best, worst ______?"[7] You can insert a word of your choosing into the blank. Some of my favorites are "day," "gift," "vacation," "friend," "date," "kiss," "teacher," or "coach." Asking kids about the first day they remember, their last day, their best day, and their worst day opens many avenues to being known.

Third, we can loop. Especially if we are dealing with interpersonal conflict, looping is necessary. When a kid is upset, listen to why they are upset, attempt to distill what is upsetting them, repeat this back to them in less than thirty seconds, and then check your understanding.[8] Here is an example of something that might have occurred in my home. Disclaimer: I am not great at looping, and what follows is what I wish I would always do in these circumstances, rather than jumping immediately to trying to fix problems, which is my typical response.

It was late one night, and my oldest daughter was spiraling. "I do not have all my homework done, and I do not feel like I have any good friends, and I am probably going to fail my test tomorrow, and you and Mom always want me to do everything perfectly, and Grace [goat-bleating sister] never does anything around the house, and you do not see everything that I do . . ." This list went on and on as we descended into tearful anxiety.

As her dad, I am potentially responsible for about 13 percent of this angst, but the percentage does not matter. I need to listen, distill, repeat, and check. Sadly, I cannot say I did this. But if I had distilled what I heard, I would have said, "Being seventeen is hard. You seem to be saying that you do not feel like you measure up, and you feel your value is primarily based on your performance. Is that right?" Instead of getting defensive or being dismissive, I am now entering into her struggle by trying to better understand. If she says, "That is not right," then I get to ask, "What would be a better description?" I need to listen well here, because this is where my genuine curiosity about her answer will result in learning for me. While they might not seem like it at the time, these conversations are a gift to parents and kids.

Fourth, we need to use the mute button. Just like a device's button meant to silence our sound, we need to employ this as we draw out others' stories. We need to create space for kids to share. The reason we might share a story is to open the space for others to share their stories. Once their stories begin, we need to listen well.

One rule that feels like it is almost universal for kids sharing meaningful or hard things is that their timing will never be convenient. That means we need to be ready to listen when they are ready to share. We do not need to offer advice or fix things immediately. Kids need at least ten times as much listening as advice. I almost always jump to advice too soon. I need to remember the mute button, and when I do speak, it needs to be a question. The question needs to come from curiosity and not advice phrased as a question. Advice phrased as a question sounds like judgment to a kid and will typically shut them down.

KIDS' OWN STORIES MATTER THE MOST

We can certainly tell kids stories about how we have grown or even how we have seen them grow, but kids benefit the most from telling their own stories. Kids have great stories inside them; they just need a few tricks for telling those stories well to themselves and others.[9] If they can become better storytellers, then they can help others move past insecurity to a more satisfying life with others.

First, kids need to tell their own stories. This does not mean they are ever the hero of the story. No one wants to hear a story where the teller is a hero.[10] We, as adults, need to model this; we need to stop selling hero narratives and start sharing stories of hope that are grounded in shared reality.

Second, kids' stories need to be memorable.[11] To navigate a complex world, our brains do everything they can to simplify input. Storytellers must give listeners a reason to pay attention, or the listeners' "lazy brain" kicks in and tells them, *I have heard this before*, or *I know how this ends*. They should lean into stories of tenacity, glimpses of purpose, or places where they have understood that they matter to others. To honor listeners, storytellers need to be as succinct as possible, create suspense, and help listeners to care. This is really hard for kindergartners, who seem to have a near-universal ability to transform a two-minute story into a seventeen-minute run-on sentence by abusing the phrase "and then." Developmentally, kindergartners might not be able to craft a succinct story, but the rest of us can give it a try!

Third, kids need to create mental movies for other kids through the stories they tell. Movies collapse and expand time. The key is that the story must keep moving. Pauses cause the lazy brain to kick in and fill in gaps or check out. We need to teach them to keep the story moving. We do that best by modeling stories that shift our perspective or demonstrate moments of insight.

If you want to see these rules applied, go back to the art story in chapter 3. This is my story, about the hero Mrs. Taylor, where I have attempted to make you care about what happens to me and kids like me in three scenes: the art room, the hall, and the first-grade classroom. The turn in the story happens when Mrs. Taylor breaks adult code and tells me Mrs. Crabtree was wrong, and I am okay. The purpose of telling a story like this is to draw others out, particularly kids, so that we can seek *their* stories.

We want to put kids on a trajectory for joy. The problem is that we cannot really "put" them on a trajectory. Their lives and their stories *are* the trajectory. When they are able to tell their own stories of adversity, belonging, and curiosity, they are on the path toward joy. We did not put them there. They found their own footing and their own way by finding their own stories. If our brains are wired for and with stories, then this might be the most crucial element to unleash a more joyful next generation. When they find their stories, they will find joy—as long as they can find purpose and hope behind the adversity that makes an experience a story.

Here is a side benefit to helping kids own their stories: Life is a lot more interesting and joyful for us as well. Hearing my children tell their own stories—even the ones where I might have been part of the adversity at the center of the story—is what feeds my gritty optimism that the world can be better.

As we'll see in the next chapter, if we get the story right, we can stop pushing self-care culture on kids and liberate them to tell a better story.

TAKEAWAY

Kids need to find and tell their own true stories. When they do, they change the trajectory of their lives.

TRY THIS

Conduct a quick appraisal:

- How vulnerable are you with the young people you serve?
- How good are you at asking questions that elicit their stories?
- How well do you loop when you are in conflict with a young person?
- How well do you use the mute button, especially when it is inconvenient or you want to defend yourself?

Which of these four questions are you best at? Do more of that!

Which of these four questions needs the most work? Consider putting something in place to make you try to use the mute button, loop, ask good questions, or be vulnerable this week.

9

STOP PUSHING SELF-CARE CULTURE ON KIDS

What is your reaction to the title of this chapter?

You might be offended and believe only a grumpy human being, probably a boomer, would write this. He's the kind of guy who wants to return to a world of "suck it up and stop whining" and will now proceed to mansplain how we should live.[1]

If your thoughts were going this direction, I do not blame you. I have heard all of this, and I am grateful to hear others' perspectives and first impressions. But I assure you, this chapter is not a recommendation to transform everyday life into boot camp or a call to neglect our human needs for some greater collective good.

Certainly, we need to care for ourselves by attending to how we eat, sleep, relate, feel, and think, so we can be emotionally, relationally, mentally, and spiritually healthy. Most members of my family, including myself, have benefited from therapy, attending to these needs, and setting boundaries. Previous generations have underemphasized attention to some or all of these aspects.

I am by no means saying that self-care is wrong. It is our job as humans to manage ourselves well and intentionally meet our own needs so we can function at full capacity. For moms and dads who exert all of their energy on the needs of others, self-care is a must. Adults and kids need to take responsibility for their own well-being. If they do not, they will not be able to participate in a flourishing community.

My point is this: In the United States, we are pushing a culture of self-care on kids that they see and enact as self-focus. If self-care becomes exclusive focus on self, they will not find joy—circumstantial happiness for a time, maybe, but not joy.

The widespread endorsement of a lifestyle overemphasizing self and overprioritizing our own comfort and preferences is partly due to a confusion about what self-care is.

WHAT SELF-CARE IS AND ISN'T

For many of us, the term *self-care* has been used so much that its meaning has expanded to "just focus on yourself and do what feels good." Defining self-care this way has at least two problems. First, we isolate ourselves. Second, we blur self-comfort with self-care.

Certainly, there is nothing wrong with some time to yourself with a couch, blanket, popcorn, and a streaming service of your choice at the end of a day to provide some comfort. But at the end of *The Office* episode—or six episodes—whatever was causing you distress will still be there. As much as I want to believe Jim and Pam can be my friends, they are stuck inside the screen in Scranton, Pennsylvania.

Even the world's biggest proponents of self-care and Zen mindfulness would agree that self-care is not about comfort. The First Noble

Truth of Buddhism is, "Life involves suffering."[2] Most world religions acknowledge this. Islam venerates suffering as a way to achieve eternal rewards. Christianity is built on a God who sent His Son to suffer in our place for our joy. Atheists also celebrate those who suffer and sacrifice for others to advance humanitarian causes or care for nature.

How much does this resemble the ways we hear self-care language used?

RaQuel Hopkins, an influential mental health and human resources expert, has asserted that our society has begun to use "mental health language as a shield." If someone says, "My mental health is not right at the moment" or "Don't talk to me because I am having a bad day," that mental health language becomes a shield and a license to focus only on themselves.

"People can name everything and not carry anything," Hopkins said. When we label everything or create boundaries around ourselves with self-care speak, we diminish the lives we are living and ultimately may not even address the stated self-care goals, whatever they might be. "Life doesn't shrink us, our refusal to face life is what shrinks us," Hopkins concluded.[3]

Do we want to steer kids toward choices that "shrink" them and "diminish" their lives?

Self-care was never meant to be a method for trying to avoid or minimize adversity. Hopkins believes that mental health is not about comfort; it's about capacity.

We want our kids to live expansive, meaningful, fulfilling lives. While kids need to learn to set healthy boundaries on their time, commitments, and relationships, we do not want them to just cope with the world in a way that makes them constantly comfortable. We want them to learn how to have hard conversations, serve others, and take strategic risks with and for others.

Simply put, expansive lives require our kids to move beyond themselves.

AI CAN LEAD TO SMALL LIVES

The first question we often ask when faced with a problem now, due to tech companies' influence on society, is, "Can AI help with that?" Advertisements for Claude, the AI tool developed by Anthropic, claim that there "has never been a worse time to be a problem."

While I do love this sentiment, AI will not be the answer to reducing self-focused self-care.

To me, spending twelve hours a day eyes glued to a small screen is the definition of a small life. This is true for all of us. Increasingly we rely on chatbots for diagnoses, comfort, and companionship.[4] We used to have to go to WebMD to get scared about an ache, a discoloration, or a sensation. Now we can communicate with AI, which has been trained to affirm and draw out more information. Some have even gone so far as to deify AI in pursuit of the singularity—the point at which AI becomes smarter than humans—to imagine a utopian world.[5]

Kids' interaction with AI feels private because it is just them and a screen, but this is a scary fallacy because the chatbot retains everything kids share. AI is appealing because it is unable to be judgmental, always available, and always affirming. Ultimately, it can act as a mirror to the already self-focused tendencies of kids who are seeking status and insights into themselves. Chatbots, however, have even gone as far as suggesting ways to self-harm, ways to hide evidence of self-harm, and methods of suicide.[6]

When kids turn to the mirror of AI, which is designed to adapt to the information it is provided, kids get a distorted view of what is probable, because that is all AI can do. AI is here, and its influence will certainly grow. Given how ubiquitous self-care is on Reddit and other online portals used to train large language models, kids will likely turn to chatbots instead of parents, peers, or other adults who know them.

What humans need is other humans. Humans are capable of emotion, intuition, imagination, and common sense. AI can only tell kids what is probable. Humans can imagine what is possible. When we share our struggles with others, their narrative intelligence—the ability to think in stories—can help unleash our stories that fuel courage and perseverance.[7]

As parents, we can lean into wisdom that requires humans. A wisdom that comes from having known a precious child since birth. A wisdom that comes from understanding context: home, community, and school. A wisdom that comes from love.

As teachers and coaches, we probably spend more time with the next generation in a given day than their parents. We have to help kids understand their stories and live life alongside them in ways that guide them with wisdom—wisdom that sees them, identifies strengths and weaknesses, and tells another human who we see them becoming.

Helping young people understand that the world does not revolve around them is a gift to them! When they feel that their value is in their performance on a travel volleyball team, on a dance team, in a classroom, on a test, or even in how they please us, no amount of self-focus will help bring them out of that misconception. The world is vast and allows us to create, collaborate, and enjoy life—without being dependent on us to continue spinning. We all benefit when we realize that the world is much bigger than the screen in our hands and the gray matter between our ears. The young people around us need us to help them experience that and remember it.

Our kids do not need to see the world from space or even from an airplane to understand their place in the world. If our kids have flown, they will have heard the warning from the flight attendant about what to do in case the cabin depressurizes. We are always to put on our own masks first before helping others—a fair point when thinking about self-care. Instead of telling our kids to take care of themselves by putting on their own masks when life's metaphorical airplane cabin depressurizes, let's help them think about who else might help them put on their masks when they are struggling.[8]

Brené Brown calls those people our "square squad"—the short list of people we can include on a Post-it Note who will show up for us and tell us the truth in love even when we don't want to hear it.[9] Our kids need to know that the best way to find a square squad is to be on others' square squads, which means looking outside of themselves. Sometimes kids need their square squads, and sometimes they just need to go out and serve someone else.

When my daughter Grace began believing things about herself that were not true, one of the best things she did was begin to muck stalls at a place where kids with disabilities rode horses. She got outside of herself, literally and figuratively. She also needed to pay attention to how she slept, ate, exercised, and attended to her emotional and spiritual life.

Here are three examples from coaching, parenting, and teaching that will help young people care for themselves by understanding that their lives are better when lived for and with others.

A DIFFERENT WAY TO COACH

I wanted to see if it was possible for a coach to encourage young people, some of whom are making seven figures, to care for themselves by caring for others, so I interviewed Coach Scott Drew, who coaches Baylor's men's basketball and won the 2021 National Championship. He took over the program in 2004 after a player killed another team member and the program received a ten-year penalty from the NCAA. Taking over the worst job in Division I college basketball required faith—a faith that informs his leadership—but the practices relating to focusing on others are universally applicable.

I was waiting outside his office when Coach Drew arrived. He put his arm around my shoulder and said, "I am sorry I am late. I pulled a hammy running a wheel route with my son. I've got to remember I can't run the wheel route anymore!"

The week before, I was in a hospital room with a friend when Coach Drew walked in, announcing, "I got my favorite keto snacks for my keto friend here," then unpacked eight different meat snacks.

The point is, when Coach Drew enters a room, he brings energy that radiates to others because he lives for others. This energy is a primary reason why he is one of the most respected coaches in college basketball.

He preaches, and I do mean preaches, a culture of J.O.Y.—Jesus, Others, Yourself. Note where "yourself" is placed.

"How do you lead a tremendously successful basketball program with athletes who might not share your faith?" I asked him.

"They know this is how we are going to care for them," was his answer. He described how the athletes can count on having a coaching staff that puts the athletes before themselves in all they do and even brings the athletes into their others-focused lifestyle.

"We start every basketball practice sharing how we have served others, what we are grateful for, and then we pray," Coach Drew said.

I cannot imagine another major college basketball program starting practice this way. Baylor's coaches build up their athletes by focusing on others. Coach Drew cares deeply about winning, but the culture he has built treats winning as a symptom of the culture rather than the primary objective. With nearly five hundred wins and a national championship under his belt, Coach Drew has found the success that other coaches crave by using this unconventional approach. More concerned with enhancing the athletes' capacity than emphasizing their comfort, the staff is continually leading them into big lives.

BIG BROTHER—LITTLE BROTHER

What if we could move kids from self-focus to life-giving focus on others? What if we could do that with kids with disabilities in middle school?

A school in Hamilton, New Zealand, has taken a step in that direction with middle-school students who are sometimes marginalized. As we all know from our own experiences, middle-school students are preoccupied with building and maintaining status, sometimes to the detriment of others. For students with special learning needs or physical disabilities, this can be especially challenging.

Students with significant needs often have a teacher's aide who follows them throughout their day. Not unlike in the United States, in New Zealand, that aide has typically been a middle-aged person who was kind and nurturing. While valuable, having a parent-type presence does little to elevate students in the eyes of their peers.

Shaun Brooker, a rugby-player-turned-educator, was leading the school and struggling to find staff to support some of their students with disabilities. Somewhat by chance, he found an ingenious and low-cost solution for raising status and caring for others. The benefits are rippling across campus.

His son, Reuben, a graduate of the school and a six foot six high-school basketball legend, needed a part-time job while attending university. One of Shaun's middle-school students, Sam,[10] who was in a wheelchair, was not performing to his potential in class and was somewhat withdrawn from other students. For twelve hours a week, they paired Sam and Reuben together.

Reuben helped Sam with his academic work and spent recess with Sam and other students. He was not supervising, but playing basketball and connecting with kids, and more importantly, connecting kids with Sam.

Shaun said, "Sam has a sense of belonging and pride because of this person walking beside him instead of another parent-like figure. He loved it. He had this posture change, he wasn't speaking back to the teacher aide, and the volume of work he was producing we hadn't seen before."

Shaun extended the program to other eighteen-to-twenty-two-year-olds who needed part-time and even full-time work. They named the program *Tuakana Teina*, which is Māori for "Big Brother–Little Brother."

Unlike in the United States, where these kinds of programs happen after school, by embedding the program into the school day, Shaun was able to help students gain status, increase engagement at school, and produce better work.

"Reuben would come home and tell me about work that Sam was doing, and he shared that with great pride," Shaun said.

Both Reuben and Sam had enhanced self-worth—not through isolation and intensified self-focus, but by focusing on others. They are living big lives as a result.

"DON'T BE BASIC—BE SLAYSIC"

On July 4, 2025, the Guadalupe River in the Texas Hill Country rose twenty-six feet in forty-five minutes, killing twenty-seven campers and counselors at Camp Mystic. All told, the flood caused at least 136 deaths.

While Lisa Arrington, a local school leader, was watching fireworks that evening, someone called her to report that one of the missing girls was a student from her school named Mary Kate. The next day, they found out she had died. She was eight years old.

Planning the opening of school after summer break and welcoming back surviving students felt deeply unfair to Lisa. The rest of the school community had heavy hearts, many of them feeling guilty for excitement about a new school year, because Mary Kate would not be there.

They found that the only way to navigate the loss was with others. School staff found joy watching security video footage of one of Mary Kate's classmates leaving flowers and a card at the school gate. Administrators opened campus during the quiet weeks of summer for all students who needed support. School leaders put out art supplies and tables, encouraging them to leave pink bows and flowers in Mary Kate's memory. They caught glimpses of joy emerging through the suffering because they were navigating it together.

Like many eight-year-old girls, Mary Kate was a certified Swiftie and obsessed with slime. Friendship bracelets and homemade slime concoctions graced the memorial tables teachers set up. Stuffed animals and cards piled up, and one teacher drew a portrait of Mary Kate.

The school community also came together for a celebration of Mary Kate's life. People recalled Mary Kate as pure light, creativity, and humor, telling jokes with a huge smile. The room, mostly filled with kids, erupted in laughter when a school leader shared one of Mary Kate's favorite phrases: "Don't be basic—be SLAYsic."

Lisa said, "I felt something inside me release and let go, and I knew that with God and with each other, we could begin the school year and find joy, not in spite of Mary Kate, but because of her."

No one would have blamed Lisa if she had said she needed to isolate herself due to her grief. But because she chose to navigate the loss with others—not merely turn inward to her own pain—she found a clear path forward for herself, helped others walk it with her, and deepened her joy through Mary Kate's memory.

Whenever we make choices like this, we live life for and with others in the hope that those relationships extend beyond our wild and precious lives situated in a fragile, achingly beautiful world.

Coach Drew, Reuben and Sam, and Lisa all display that the best way to care for kids is to help them get outside of themselves. It is on us to help them care for themselves by understanding that their lives are better when lived for and with others. We can think of this as changing the focus of our pictures from selfies to ussies, or better yet, pictures of the people and world around us.

BIG LIVES

As kids live big, outward-facing lives, they are, of course, bound to have tough moments, and it can be tempting for adults to turn to overly protective precautions. Trigger warnings are an example of how we try to protect people, particularly kids, from things that might affect their mental health. Maybe we think of them as a societal form of self-care to keep people from being traumatized or retraumatized by content.

But what does the research say about trigger warnings?

They do not affect emotional responses; instead, they increase anticipation and might increase engagement with negative material.[11]

As adults try to use mental health language, self-care speak, and trigger warnings as shields to protect kids, we in fact do the opposite. We shrink their lives with overly protective language and practices. We tap their curiosity to see what they have been warned not to look at—we all know that if you want a teenager to look at something, just tell them not to.

So, using mental health language as a shield diminishes opportunities to build capacity. Focusing on self-care separates kids from others and shrinks their lives. Trigger warnings might not protect kids. In fact, they might just be an effective way to suck them into negative material. While we need to protect kids from trauma, we need to be thoughtful about what is most effective. And we can't get in the way of them learning that life will be full of adversity and that this can be a gift when experienced with others.

Schools should be places where kids lean into adversity every day when they do hard things with their classmates. Sometimes the school itself changes the way a neighborhood experiences adversity. St. Augustine Preparatory Academy (Aug Prep) is a school on the south side of Milwaukee with over 2,200 students, 98 percent of whom are students of color and 86 percent of whom are economically disadvantaged. Annually, the school scores in the top 1 percent for academic growth in the state of Wisconsin. Like many great schools, kids graduate and go on to elite universities, amazing careers, and lives well-lived.

What is special about Aug Prep is that it has also changed a community. When the school opened in 2017, the crime rate in the neighborhood dropped by 43 percent. School leaders have big dreams and are opening another campus on the north side of the city.

Big lives are built with others. That is great news because joy is found in the overflow of enduring love and made evident in a life lived for others. We are made to love others, and when we do, we can see the way we are loved reflected back to us. People who are loved are more loving. This does not mean that everything will be easy. In fact, big lives focused on others will be hard. There are times when we will need self-comfort, but sometimes self-care isn't really about the self at all.

Take the remedy for seasickness as a metaphor for how we live for joy with others. If our kids are starting to feel queasy, the best thing we can do when life starts rocking back and forth is tell them what any sailor knows: "Keep your eyes up and out." Focusing on a point on the horizon, up and away from self and present distress, is the best way to care for ourselves when adversity comes.

TAKEAWAY

Sometimes self-care becomes self-comfort and can be a hideout from struggle. When we hide, we disconnect ourselves from joy. Self-care is not care when its end is self-focus.

TRY THIS

Take a look at yourself.

- When do you need self-comfort (e.g., mindless streaming, Ben & Jerry's, or a salty snack)?
- When do you need self-care?

- What are examples of how self-care enables you to move beyond yourself and into a big life of impact?
- When does self-care mean you need to focus on others?

Now ask a few kids you support:

- When do you turn to self-comfort?
- What do you do that is productive self-care?
- How are those two approaches working?
- What do you do to focus on others that brings joy?

PART 3

A HOSPITABLE WELCOME TO A BETTER WAY

We have made it to the best part of the book. Part 3 is the invitation to a better way to live. We are not trying to get kids to "buy in" to a better life. We are inviting them to co-own a great life with others.

To launch the next generation into a more joyful future, we will engage their hearts and minds in ways that move beyond being comfortable (chapter 10). Sometimes we will even push engagement to the point that the risks feel unsafe, particularly for kids who might be marginalized, but we will celebrate the risks that they take (chapter 11). Often, that celebration comes in the form of hospitality, which moves beyond mere service. Instead of dutiful lives of service, we invite young people into hospitable living, where they know they matter to us and others (chapter 12).

Because we are inviting others into a better way to live, this book does not really end; instead, we launch more joyful lives. Joy is not a destination that we measure progress against—that would actually erode joy. Joy is a celebration of growth, and in the final chapter, we will invite kids into this process (chapter 13). If we live life with others, we will find the joy that comes along the way and will stop worrying about ephemeral, ill-defined success.

Inviting kids into adversity is hard.

Inviting them into joy is easier.

We have to do both.

The invitation must communicate to them that they matter and that there is joy in a life that matters. I am extending the invitation to joy to you, so you can extend that invitation to others who matter to you.

10

OUR JOB IS NOT TO MAKE KIDS COMFORTABLE

Consider how familiar or reasonable the following two scenarios sound to you.

Parent in the after-school hours: "Middle-school kids are so self-centered that we cannot expect them to talk to us. It's not in their nature. They need some time to decompress in their rooms with their phones, so we let them have a couple of hours to themselves to connect with friends on video games or on social media."

Read, "We really have no idea what they do in their rooms or for how long."

Professor at the beginning of class: College students enter the room. The professor asks, "What is your energy today? Do you feel like engaging in class? Give me a thumbs-up or thumbs-down. For those of you who put your thumbs down, if you need some personal headspace, take some time for yourself. As you know, I will not call on you unless you feel safe and have energy to engage."

Read, "I am willing to teach only the students who want to be here."

Can you imagine if K-12 teachers took that approach? A ninth-grade algebra teacher might have a very small class!

The adults in these scenarios mean well, but they are, in truth, failing the young people around them. Why? Because they are overly focused on comfort—both their comfort and that of the kids.

It is not our job to make kids comfortable. It is our job to engage their hearts and minds. Their job is to learn, and sometimes that is uncomfortable. True engagement occurs when students own their learning.

ENGAGEMENT > COMFORT

What if we had more people like Brad Livingstone, who moves kids beyond comfort to deep engagement?

A six foot ten giant with brilliant white hair, Brad has been a high-school teacher for decades in California, Virginia, and Texas. With a specialty in World War II, he has a classroom that could be a military museum, with model planes hanging from the ceiling and helmets, uniforms, flags, and pictures displayed in cases.

Like any great history teacher, he makes classes come alive with these incredible artifacts and engaging readings, stories, and guest speakers. When veterans visit his classes to share their experiences, Brad trains his students how to listen and ask good questions of a fading generation. Louis Zamperini, the subject of the book and movie *Unbroken*, was a guest speaker in Brad's classroom when he was in his eighties—and even raced two of Brad's track athletes down the hall during his visit.

History comes to life in Brad's classroom. More importantly, the students become more than spectators; they become active agents of the present and future based on their understanding of the past.

When I had the privilege of sitting in on one of Brad's classes, I heard students reporting numbers to Brad, which he then recorded in a notebook.

"I got two," said a student.

"I got one," reported another.

"I got seventeen," someone else shared.

This continued until all the students had entered the room.

I happened to be sitting next to the student whose number was seventeen. I asked him, "You said, 'I got seventeen.' What did you mean?"

"We keep track of how many veterans we thank for their service each week and then report that every Monday morning," he explained.

"How did you find seventeen veterans?"

"That was easy," he replied. "I just watched for people who saluted the flag at the football game on Friday night, and then I went and thanked them for their service during the game."

I was completely dumbfounded. How does a teacher build a culture where students will use the Friday night lights of a Texas football game to strategically scan the crowd to find a veteran to thank?

I asked Brad how he pushed kids out of their comfort zones so they engage their communities with civic gratitude.

"At the beginning of every school year, we go to H-E-B [local grocery store] at lunchtime," he told me. "I split students up into pairs and have them look for older men and women in the store. I tell them to introduce themselves and ask them if they have served in the military. If they have, the students thank them for their service."

His students have never found less than ten in those training visits to the store.

"Some students are anxious about doing this, but when they come back, most are ready to go do it on their own," Brad added.

Each semester, the class has a goal to thank one thousand veterans for their service. When a student thanks fifty veterans, Brad gives the student a vial of sand from the beaches of Normandy. The student who thanks the most veterans over the course of the semester receives a vial of sand from Iwo Jima. Brad calls this sand the "most exclusive soil on earth" because you have to be a member of the Japanese military, or a U.S. military attaché to the Japanese military, to even get to the volcanic island.

A year later, I was able to observe Brad's class interact with Ed Newman, a one-hundred-year-old WWII veteran. Each student walked up to him, shook his hand, and said some variation of "Thank you for coming today, Mr. Newman. We are so glad you are here. Thank you for your service."

For the next hour, Ed humbly shared his story as students asked question after question. Homeless and out of school at the age of twelve, Ed traveled from city to city with his fourteen-year-old brother looking for work.

"Back then, they didn't really ask your age," said Ed. "They just checked if you were big enough and could do the work."

Ed joined the U.S. Navy the day he turned seventeen and was on an aircraft carrier in the Pacific ten weeks later. Because he had previously worked as a baker, he was assigned to the bakery. When under attack, he manned his battle station with a 20mm gun.

As he spoke with a scratchy voice and gestured with hands gnarled by arthritis, the students were mesmerized. They leaned forward to hear this man withered by time, aware of how increasingly unique this opportunity was to learn from a WWII veteran from the Greatest Generation.

They wanted to know what Ed had done on the ship in his free time.

"Poker. I was pretty good. And boxing—I had a friend who was an amateur boxer," was the answer.

"What are you most proud of from your time in the war?" one student asked respectfully.

Ed paused, then responded, "I made sure the boys got fed and enjoyed their food. Whatever that ship did, I had a part in that."

The final question that came from a student was, "Do you have any wisdom for us?"

"Do what you're doing," Ed replied. "Get that schoolin'. Follow your nose. Whatever you do, you gotta make a livin'."

At the end of the class period, the entire class surrounded Ed for a group picture, then individuals wanted additional pictures. The students thanked him again for his class visit and for his service. They treated him like the hero that he was. They had been engaged in a class period that might stick with them for the rest of their lives. I know it will for me.

When we engage kids instead of just thinking about their comfort, they can change the communities around them. If Brad would have stopped at what makes kids comfortable, most never would have thanked a veteran. Imagine how different communities would be if they were filled with respectful teenagers who thanked the people who have served so that they can be free.

ENGAGEMENT > COMPLIANCE

While comfort is not the goal, compliance isn't either. No one really wants to just comply; both adults and kids want freedom within boundaries.

To be clear, compliance is better than chaos. We have all seen teams, classrooms, and homes that could benefit from some basic compliance that would deliver them from anarchy. But we don't want to go to the extreme of kids dutifully, mindlessly following the direction of an adult.

Kids who are especially compliant wait to be told what to do next, have little agency, and struggle to develop into problem-solving, critically thinking adults. While compliance is all boundaries, engagement provides freedom within boundaries.

As parents, we want our kids to use judgment that becomes wisdom by testing how to interact with others and the world. Freedom within boundaries is the purpose of curfews, time limits on devices, and clear expectations for school. Kids feel safe in these kinds of environments—not safe just to be comfortable and complacent, but safe to take strategic risks.

I love walking into a high-school physics classroom where students are testing, hypothesizing, and tracking data. I am always impressed by homes where kids greet us at the door, sit at a meal, and ask and answer questions. While these skills have been cultivated by parents, the kids seem to be genuinely engaged and curious.

Engagement means that kids own what they are doing. They want to understand the physical world better in a lab. They want to know the people around them when they are welcomed into homes. They are deeply curious. Compliance can crush curiosity. Engagement fuels curiosity.

There is, however, a range of what constitutes engagement that moves beyond mere compliance. That range is dependent on each kid. Some kids, like my oldest daughter, are very comfortable with compliance. As a teenager, Sarah told me, "I am not a fan of autonomy. I prefer to have an adult with my best interest in mind tell me what to do." Most of the time, she was more than happy to comply. Sarah needed a push beyond her comfort zone, which came with going off to college and then studying in a foreign country.

As for our other two kids, let's just say they have never been looking for an adult to tell them what to do.

What Sarah needs is different from what her siblings need. This requires us to know each kid well and recognize that they will develop uniquely and will need different boundaries at different times. Sometimes they need a push, and sometimes they need a tightened boundary. The key is to know each kid. This is hard to do in the world in which many of us currently live.

What would it look like if parents and kids spent time together each night, not out of compliance, but to engage with one another, rather than passively looking at screens in different rooms?

ENGAGEMENT > ENTERTAINMENT

That last question was not meant to be a shot across the bow! For my family, it sometimes feels like a win to get us all in one room watching the same screen. I had one college student recently share that she "triple screens" most of the time because she has two different games she "is addicted to" that she plays on her phone and iPad simultaneously while she watches Netflix with friends on a larger screen.

The point is that engagement is different from entertainment. Triple screening sounds exhausting and is about a very low level of distracting entertainment. In no way can that student be engaged in any one of her screens, much less with anyone in the room. We live in an ecosystem that actively fights deep engagement in the real world with digital pacifiers.

As parents and educators, we are fighting an uphill battle on this front—a battle in which we are not doing ourselves any favors. Our kids' expectations are being set by a world that has turned them into products, commodities, and users—and we gave the world this access. By age two, four in ten kids have their own digital tablets. By age eight, over half of kids have their own mobile devices.[1] Kids are absorbing a warped view of what happiness is when they think it is just a click away.

As parents, my wife and I could certainly have done a better job moving beyond entertainment to engagement. Hearing stories like that of the Baskins is a good reminder of that.

Jake Baskin grew up in a home where screen time was very limited, and he had two options when he was not doing chores or at school: read or go outside. Meredith Baskin came from a family with unlimited screen time. She spent much of her free time in her bedroom reading because family time often centered on the television, and while she craved personal interaction, she found more satisfaction in books. When Jake and Meredith got married, they decided they would not have a television in their home. If your sensibilities are as offended as mine, please keep reading, and know that I see you!

Today they have four kids, ranging in age from seven to eleven, and they still do not have a television in their house, though they do have occasional family movie nights using their laptops. The kids do not have personal screens; instead, they read, play creatively, or go outside. They read a lot of books, many of them aloud, and find the adventures that "bored" kids find in an outdoor world filled with wonder.

Jake and Meredith have said they will revisit the possibility of incorporating television and screens when the kids get older. For now, their kids have tapped into the joy of curiosity and belonging that exists in a family that emphasizes reading and the outdoors.

Isn't that a more joyful way to live than triple screening?

I am not saying that all screens are bad and are the only impediment to good parenting or adventurous lives. We have screens in our home and have loved family movie nights and watching sports for years. We also have enjoyed having students and friends over to watch games and shows countless times. But I do wonder if our family would have been more joyful if we had spent less time with screens and more time reading and being outside. I am hard-pressed to think we wouldn't have been.

Your kids might want to rip these pages out of the book; they might even be chanting, "Don't take our screens!" Taking away screens is not the point. Inviting kids into deeper engagement is.

When it comes to learning, we don't prioritize entertainment. We prioritize engagement—with ideas, skills, and other people. Sometimes engagement means we are going to do hard things, developing the muscles around the backbone that will prepare us to do even more challenging things in the future. Sometimes engagement is just more fun than passive entertainment.

The student who shared her triple-screen practices was at our house with eight other students for dinner and a night of questions. Stemming from a discussion in my leadership capstone course, students asked if they could come over for dinner one night and spend the evening asking each other questions like these:[2]

- What would constitute a perfect day for you?
- What makes you apprehensive about leaving Baylor?
- What is your life story in four minutes?
- If you knew that in five years you would die suddenly, would you change anything about the way you are living now? Why?

I did not have to compel them to come, to eat together, or to put screens away. We just invited one another into deeper engagement. We are wired for this. Engagement leads to being seen, known, and loved.

What would it look like if we spent more time asking questions and a little less time on cat videos?

REWIRING FOR DEEPER CONNECTION

In recent years state governments have been taking the initiative to improve conditions for meaningful engagement in schools. In possibly one of the most remarkable policy developments of the millennium, California, New York, and Texas actually agree about something. All three have passed legislation banning phones in schools. In 2025 alone, twenty-two states passed new laws to restrict phone use in schools.[3]

After the phones disappeared, educators in these states reported improved student relationships, louder cafeterias, and less drama. One principal of a 2,600-student high school recently told me, "I was skeptical when the legislature said we had to ban phones, but I have to say, there is a lot less drama. Phones being gone has been a blessing."

This principal was surprised that students adapted. Why? Because phone use provides a comfort zone for kids, and adults have been conditioned to believe that kids just want to be comfortable.

I am increasingly convinced that is not what they really want, even if they do not have the awareness or ability to articulate it. We all might need a break from phones to rewire our brains for deeper, more human connection. Recent data showing a shift in engagement in schools seems to support this. A massive study of seventeen thousand students in India demonstrated that going phone-free during class substantially improved student grades.[4] Another study in

Florida demonstrated that phone-free classrooms improved learning and decreased unexcused absences.[5]

According to Jean Twenge, one of the leading experts on technology and young people, students and adults are completely distracted by their devices.[6] One in four teenagers admits to seeing pornography during the school day, and almost half saw it on a school-issued device.[7] Even if they are not looking at porn, teenagers are at least as distracted as college students who report spending nearly 40 percent of *class time* on social media, emails, and videos![8] From elementary to college, reading on paper rather than digitally leads to better comprehension.[9] This does not feel like a complicated fix for schools: less virtual world and more real world.

Here is more empirical evidence to support this intuitive understanding. In a study of almost three hundred thousand students in fourth through eighth grade, those who spent more time on devices in language arts class performed worse on reading tests.[10] College students who took handwritten notes were 58 percent more likely to get A's in classes than those who typed notes on laptops.[11] Benefits to handwriting begin early, with children learning basic reading skills significantly better when they write rather than type letters.[12] Neuroscience findings confirm that handwriting is an important tool for learning.

In a study of thirteen-to-eighteen-year-olds in the United States, 78 percent say that they have at least one teacher who makes them excited about the future—an 8 percent increase since 2023. Of those same students, 75 percent report that someone has told them they have done good work at school—a 5 percent increase since 2023. Similarly, 66 percent of students reported learning something interesting at school in the past week, which is a 3 percent improvement over 2023.[13]

While I am still concerned about the students not reporting positive experiences, we are seeing improvement.

Humans are wired for connection with others—connection that

is strongest when it is face-to-face. What if kids just need to experience a better way of engaging with the embodied souls around them? We stop seeing people as ordinary when we start seeing who they are more deeply. As C. S. Lewis once wrote, we "have never met a mere mortal."[14] Instead of primarily resorting to a like, swipe, or share, which becomes a transactional interaction, kids need to see in-person interaction as a way to live fully. Just as seeing a picture of the Grand Canyon is wildly different from standing at its rim, screen-mediated connection is vastly different from physical presence with others. In both instances, having a real-world experience significantly enhances the likelihood of wonder, curiosity, and deeper engagement.[15]

When you have stood on the edge of the Grand Canyon, you don't want to settle for someone else's selfie there. When you are truly engaged in living life within the moment, you are not concerned about getting your selfie there either.

Are real-world adventures less safe for kids than staying in their rooms and using a screen as a portal to the world? I would argue no. Earlier in this book, we discussed the isolation, comparison, and atrophy that comes from living life through a tiny window into others' filtered, curated lives. I wouldn't call the resulting despair, sense of purposelessness, and other life-threatening troubles comfortable or safe.

As adults, we need to continue to invite young people into something better, which starts with no longer mowing the figurative lawn. When we bring kids into intellectual, physical, relational, and spiritual adventures, we might end up trekking through some tall grass—but this is a better way to live. Kids love adventures and learn to seek more of them after they have had a taste. Engaging them in adventures with us now will train them to tackle adversity and adventure with others throughout their lives.

What might this look like in different areas of young people's lives?

BETTER THAN COMFORT

Academically, welcoming kids into engagement is as simple as calling on a kid in class who hasn't raised her hand. In good classrooms, there is no shame in getting a wrong answer. Because we live in a culture where getting the answer wrong is a sign of weakness instead of an opportunity to learn, we have many kids who are anxious about being called on to answer questions they are not sure about. But if we let kids go through the day avoiding engagement in the name of their comfort, we do not give them the chance to grow.

Teachers, call on kids who do not raise their hands. Celebrate when they try even when they are wrong. Letting a kid get by with "I didn't raise my hand" or "I don't know" is not good teaching. Those kinds of responses set them on the path to poorly lived lives.

Physical challenges are relatively straightforward. Screens, isolation, and sedentary lifestyles seem to be becoming the default, so encourage kids to play, be active, and push their bodies to try new things. Real-world bruises are better than virtual scars.[16] Don't try to get them to work out. Instead, invite them to go on hikes, build something, or just run with the wind hitting their faces. Give them time to be outside with friends without interference from adults organizing things. Given the right circumstances, they will take this autonomy and run.

As they grow older, broaden the boundaries and give them increasing freedom to try new things. Eventually, those physical challenges can be enhanced and encouraged by coaches who will help kids develop their bodies so they can become more of who they are meant to be, but initially, giving them autonomy, peers, and the outdoors is probably enough.[17]

Relationally, kids benefit from exposure to peers with a wide range of personalities and cultures. They need to experience and work through conflict. Conflict is not comfortable, but it does provide remarkable opportunities to engage another's perspective. As adults, we have to stop mowing down potential conflict and let kids learn to navigate small-scale differences (which might feel like life-altering experiences to them in the moment). Certainly, there are times when we need to intervene, but given our tendencies today, those times are probably less frequent than we think.

People talk about spirituality in different ways, but this one might be new to you: What if a key to kids' spiritual engagement was boredom?

Boredom is an enemy in the classroom and can lead to disengagement. But when kids are bored outside of school—if kids have the time to be—their brains start to work differently.

Arthur Brooks has found that "being bored can lead you to ask big questions."[18] (Maybe boredom was the strategy that so many preachers in my childhood were trying to tap into for me!) According to Brooks, the explosion of depression and anxiety in modern society has resulted from people not knowing the meaning of their lives, which can be nurtured in the open, "boring" gaps of time in life.

Unfortunately, according to Brooks, we have found a way to almost completely shut down boredom. We take out our phones when we have to wait fifteen seconds at a corner or in a grocery store line. When we do this, we avoid the brain's default mode—which allows for deeper questions and thoughts—because we might find it uncomfortable. We may never get to deeper questions of meaning and purpose if we always pull out our phones. And without meaning, we can experience anxiety, depression, and a hollow life.[19]

If we want young people to have deep engagement relationally, physically, academically, and in the real world, might the path to that involve some boredom? If that gets them to the bigger questions that lead to bigger lives, then yes. So, let kids be bored (just not in school!).

PUTTING IT ALL TOGETHER

We've seen in this chapter that engagement is not about getting kids to do what the adult wants; that is compliance. It also is not about getting the adult to do what the kid wants; that is comfort and entertainment. Engagement is about adults inspiring kids to lean in *with them*, then both adults and kids finding joy in learning.

This view of engagement is a key component of how all learning occurs. At the Baylor Center for School Leadership, we believe learning is about three things: feedback, engagement, and well-being (an easy acronym to remember: FEW).

We define *feedback* as actionable wisdom for growth. In fact, we have surveyed over thirty-eight thousand kids as well as teachers, parents, and college students about student well-being, level of engagement in class, and how they grow through feedback.

Our view of *engagement* has been the focus of this chapter.

And we define *well-being* as a collective sense of respect, trust, autonomy, and efficacy.

We get to flourishing by ensuring that each kid is mentally and relationally engaged in a way that demonstrates co-ownership of the learning process.[20] We use the term *well-being* because that is what is common in schools, but what we really have in mind is flourishing. A kid might be able to be well on her own, but she needs others to flourish.

We believe these concepts apply to anyone working with kids. If you and I are prioritizing feedback, engagement, and well-being with kids effectively, joy will be part of the experience.

This does not have to be complicated. Our concept of FEW is really about living life together. The dinner with college students I mentioned earlier is a great example of all three. Feedback from students is the reason the dinner happened. They then proceeded to engage with one another as they gave all kinds of feedback on the questions that engaged them in deeper connection. Their well-being was enhanced by free food, connection with others, and conversations that spilled into the night. Three of the students stood out on the sidewalk for an hour and a half after they left, deepening their connections. In the next chapter, we explore the antidote to comfort and the kind of boredom that can lead to apathy.

TAKEAWAY

Engagement should always be the goal because it leads to joy. Don't let comfort, compliance, or entertainment get in the way.

TRY THIS

This week, put screens away for dinner. Get takeout or make a meal that everyone likes. Spend one hour just talking.

Need a starter question? Ask a young person, "If you were to die this evening with no opportunity to communicate with anyone, what would you most regret not having told someone? Why haven't you told them?"

One more thing: Answer those two questions yourself and go tell the person. Joy is on the other side!

11

KIDS SEEK STATUS, NOT SAFETYISM

In the beginning of this book, I reported that parents from all over the world tell me, "We just want our kids to be happy."

The second-most-common desire I hear from parents, especially those in the United States, is this: "We just want our kids to be safe."

Let's start with this disclaimer: Physical and psychological safety are absolute necessities for schools, homes, and workplaces. School shootings, inappropriate behavior of adults, and any kind of violence have no place in schools. Sadly, we live in a world where these things have become far too prevalent. As a reminder, I see value in kids experiencing adversity, not trauma, so their learning communities must be psychologically safe. They should be able to take interpersonal risks and know that they will not be punished for sharing concerns, asking questions, and making mistakes.[1]

In this chapter, however, I am pushing back against "safetyism," which is characterized by lawn-mower parents and educators who are obsessed with eliminating threats and providing excessive protection.

The worship of safety above everything else makes kids feel more fragile and anxious.[2] When safetyism becomes the ultimate goal, we're no longer focused on developing kids' strength and agency.

Safety provides the foundation from which kids can launch into adventures—some of which will not feel altogether safe. These types of adventures are best experienced in physically and psychologically safe places. Ask any marginalized kid who has experienced some level of success about their journey, and they will tell you their success required risk-taking that did not feel 100 percent safe. Creating the expectation in kids that they should feel safe before they contribute is similar to telling a sea turtle to leave its hole only when it is safe. That precarious journey across the sand to the sea will never feel safe!

Kids know this intuitively. And the more kids experience, the more evidence they have that it is true.

Ask any kid what their favorite roller coaster is, and they'll probably say the tallest, fastest, "most dangerous" ride they have ever ridden.

Kids want adventure, even those who are risk-averse. I was firmly in the risk-averse camp as a kid. I did not ride a real roller coaster until I was eighteen, when I found myself at Six Flags Great America with college friends. The only reason I joined the group was because I did not want to lose status. By the end of the day, I had become a roller coaster fan. My favorite ride was the tallest and fastest, Raging Bull. Though my resistance to risk remained part of my personality, I experienced the joy of adventure and belonging that came with a little danger.

My son took status-seeking well beyond roller coasters for me. In fact, he is responsible for the dumbest thing I have ever done: running with the bulls.

For the past five hundred years, people in Pamplona, Spain, have maintained a tradition of running through their ancient cobblestone streets with bulls. The San Fermín festival runs for eight days, and each morning at eight, a gun signals the release of a dozen 1,500-pound bulls into the streets, where people who have been partying all night run alongside them, trying to get as close as possible while avoiding being gored or trampled on the way to the bullring.

On our first day at the festival, we watched from a third-floor balcony overlooking what is aptly named "Dead Man's Curve." Thousands of people waited in the streets for twelve bulls to round the corner so they could run with them. Unfortunately, one man was trampled by four bulls that morning, but the combined weight of three tons of bull did not kill him. I looked over at my son to determine if the recklessness of this event had made an impression.

"That was insane, right?" I asked.

"That was awesome," he responded with eyes glowing.

Due to his underdeveloped prefrontal cortex, a condition common to all nineteen-year-olds, Ben thought it would be a great idea for the two of us to put on neckerchiefs and join in this cultural moment the next morning.

That night in the hotel room, I could not sleep. Every fiber of my risk-averse forty-eight-year-old fully developed prefrontal cortex was telling me this was a terrible idea. I had absolutely no interest in putting myself in proximity to any bulls. But would I be a horrible father if I let my son run on his own and something happened to him?

That is how I found myself in the street at 7:56 a.m. the next day, wearing my neckerchief. I recorded a seventeen-second clip of my son right before someone fired the gun to release the bulls into the street.

"How are you feeling?" I asked him in the recording.

"A little jittery," he answered. "This is real now. Let's see how this goes."

Before I stopped recording, I captured my face. I was smiling.

Parents, you know this was not a smile of happiness or joy.

Remember, I am risk-averse, and I knew this was the stupidest thing I had ever done. This smile was one of resignation. I was in this with my kid. He was an idiot, and so was I.

But were we?

In no way am I endorsing running with the bulls, bullfighting, or willingly putting your kids in harm's way. Even so, Ben and I will never forget that day. We ran the fastest quarter mile of our lives and hurdled multiple people on the way to the arena. When we got to the bullring, I made another short recording, panning the arena filled with twenty thousand people in the stands.

"How are you feeling now?" I asked Ben.

"Exhilarated!" he exclaimed.

I followed up with a brief description to the camera: "That was insane."

Life is exhilarating and insane in so many ways. You do not have to run with the bulls with your kids to know this. If you have driving-age kids, you have probably experienced the moment on the interstate when your kid holds both of your lives in her hands as she is going seventy miles per hour in between two semis. In that moment, you have trusted your life to a person who once needed training wheels and your supportive hand on her bicycle seat to stay upright. Together you are in a situation that, statistically, is far more dangerous than riding roller coasters or running with the bulls in Pamplona.[3]

UNDERDEVELOPED BRAIN OR STATUS-SEEKING?

I attributed Ben's desire to run with the bulls to his underdeveloped prefrontal cortex, but that is only partially correct. Ben, as a nineteen-year-old, was seeking status.

Starting at around the age of ten, both boys and girls experience significant increases in testosterone as they start moving toward puberty. Researchers have demonstrated that increased testosterone makes kids more sensitive to what gives them status among peers and adults. Therefore, they purposefully do things that elevate themselves in the eyes of others.[4] They seek the praise of those they believe to be praiseworthy. Even kids who say, "I don't care what other people think" really do care.

When we immediately attribute kids' illogical behavior to the "neurobiological incompetence model" (e.g., kids do stupid things because they do not think), we overlook how they are seeking to be valued by peers and adults.[5] If status, even more than an underdeveloped caution center in the brain, is what causes kids to take risks, then we need to shift the way we invite kids into learning, struggle, and adventure.

No one wants to be invited into compliance-driven drudgery governed by safety-obsessed adults. If kids roughly ten and up are trying to seek status in an adult world, then safetyism will be their kryptonite, leading them to extreme frustration. Safetyism might even drive them to take even more dangerous risks to achieve status.

Throughout the rest of this chapter, we are going to take a closer look at this understandable frustration and what adults can do differently.

We need to sustain meaningful relationships with kids, hold them accountable in ways that build them into stronger people, and give them a solid foundation from which to launch.

LEAVING ROOM FOR RISK-TAKING

To develop socially and emotionally, sometimes kids need to do things that do not always feel safe. In years past, recess was one of the places where this would happen.

The 1980s in Indiana were not exactly like what is depicted in fictional Hawkins from *Stranger Things*, but there was something a bit grittier about elementary-school recess.

We played serious games of kickball on asphalt. In our kickball games, you could throw the ball at opponents as they ran the bases to "peg" them. If you hit them anywhere other than the head—we were civilized, no headshots—they were out. I once dove to catch a kickball to get a critical out, and a shard of a broken beer bottle hidden in the grass cut through my Sears "toughskin" jeans to my tibia. The cut required seven stitches, but the most important thing for me was that I did not drop the ball. That scar on my leg remains a testament to my kickball toughness.

We also played basketball year-round, even in winter coats with a layer of snow on the ground. We called our own fouls and set rules that governed all things, from who played to how long we played.

The average modern elementary-school student gets twenty-seven minutes of recess per day,[6] because many policymakers believe that less recess time will result in better academic outcomes. But the move toward less recess time for kids has not resulted in better academic outcomes, as math and reading scores are the lowest they have been in a generation.[7] We know recess advances social and emotional development; improves memory, attention, and concentration; reduces disruptive behavior; and increases physical activity.[8] A recent study even shows that recess time seems to reduce the stress hormone cortisol.[9]

Kids benefit from life lessons in the real world;[10] it's where they build lifelong skills that cannot be attained other ways. They need to encounter low-level, developmentally appropriate conflict. How long should a kid be on a swing until it is someone else's turn? What are the rules to a game? What happens when someone breaks a rule? How do we make fair teams? As adults, we should insert ourselves as little as possible in these issues, and our involvement should decrease as young people develop.

Sadly, it is common for adults today to intervene in student conflicts, with potentially devastating consequences for development. Here are three such examples from elementary schools.

In California, a school posted *nine rules* for tag on the playground fence, including a "one-finger touch" for tagging. Would anyone even know they had been tagged? That would certainly lead to controversy. No fear, there is a rule for that. Kids were to resolve disagreements with the go-to conflict-resolution tool used by the judiciary everywhere: "Rock paper scissors." Truly, the wisdom of Solomon on display.[11]

Students in Texas were having an age-old conflict about who got to be on swings and for how long. Instead of leaving it to the kids to work this out, the principal told a teacher to oversee "swing switch." The teacher had to set a timer, let kids know when their turn was over, then direct the next kid to climb on. At what age do young people get to determine how to share swings? Middle school, high school, or college?

At one school in Tennessee, students typically played soccer, basketball, and touch football at recess. When conflict arose about who was getting to play and how aggressively kids were playing, the school's solution was to take all balls away for recess. The message: If you cannot figure out how to play well together, then you won't play at all.

Recess is not meant to be free of conflict or always safe. Kids will struggle and get physically, emotionally, and socially hurt. As adults, we have to accept this as a necessary risk as kids develop the muscles around their backbones to make them resilient. I am not advocating unsupervised, no-holds-barred, law-of-the-jungle recess. Kids feel the most secure when they know they have freedom within parameters.

But we should not need posted rules for tag, adult timers for swing turns, and ball-free recess. Free time outside allows young people to engage with others in developmentally beneficial ways. In the past, kids spent far more time outdoors and found many long-term benefits outside of the direct control of adults.[12]

Across various age groups and settings, safetyism should not be impeding kids' healthy status-seeking. Young people need opportunities to take reasonable risks and negotiate their own conflicts on the way to becoming adults. Before they can manage boardrooms, courtrooms, or cubicle politics, they need to learn to navigate social interactions that might feel fraught but are developmentally appropriate proving grounds. They also just need to have fun!

This is exactly what a middle school near Vancouver, British Columbia, does, as administrators make adventure a rite of passage. They embark on an adventure with SALTS, the Sail and Life Training Society, a charity that provides youth mentorship programs at sea. For the past twenty years, every eighth grader has gone on a four-day voyage aboard a 120-foot schooner. Leaving devices behind, students and staff embark on an adventure that is equal parts adventure and hands-on training.

Students are divided into watch groups and learn to sail and maintain the ship: taking the helm, plotting courses, handling sails, keeping anchor watch, and scrubbing decks. Instruction covers knots, navigation, and the rules of the sea, but the deeper lessons come from living and working in community. Every shift demands cooperation. No one can raise a sail alone. Chores like washing dishes and cleaning the deck teach humility and service. Evenings are filled with games, songs, and storytelling on deck, and shore excursions bring moments of wonder.

There is real struggle. Many students have never spent a night away from home, and homesickness, seasickness, and fear of climbing the rigging (one hundred feet above deck) test them. Early mornings and night watches leave them exhausted. Tempers flare and patience is tested as students learn to resolve conflicts in cramped quarters.

"Tears flow at both ends of the spectrum: when their nerves fray and, later, when they don't want to return to shore," one of the school leaders, Regan Davis, reported. "Yet through the struggle a different kind of joy takes root. They discover strength and courage they didn't know they had."

He points out that students are celebrated not for who they pretend to be but for who they are. Students return more confident, empathetic, and deeply connected to other kids.

"We see joy when a group cheers each other on across the ship, or when a hesitant student climbs the rigging," Regan added. "As teachers, we have the privilege of mentoring in these moments: we offer encouragement, share truth in love when attitudes need adjusting, and model servant leadership as we haul lines alongside our students."

High schools, colleges, and employers all over the world create service opportunities, adventures, and rites of passage that help bring young people into community. Going through hard things like SALTS, community-service projects, or induction into organizations builds bridges through opportunities that do not initially feel safe. Wilderness trips for kids who have grown up in cities or suburbs are not primarily about enjoying nature; they are about challenging young people to become more of who they are meant to be within a community of fellow travelers.

When we move beyond talking about what we want to see our kids become to living it beside them, that is when lives change—both ours and theirs.

PARENTING APPROACHES

The previous examples were all based in schools. As parents, there is even more we can do to invite kids into more joyful lives by doing things that do not feel safe, holding them to high standards, and providing appropriate support. So much of this happens in day-to-day interactions. When we stop venerating safetyism, we can help our kids seek status strategically. Let's look at a few parenting approaches that could either help or hinder our efforts.

Authoritarian parenting, which involves high expectations without support, becomes punitive parenting and could lead toward safetyism without actually being safe in the long run. "Because I said so" and "I am the adult, and you are the child" are hallmarks of this kind of parenting. When kids do not meet a parent's high expectations, the kids are punished. In a world where positional authority has diminished, this type of parenting has limited efficacy, especially as kids reach puberty and seek status.[13]

Almost half of parents report wanting to raise their kids differently from the way they were raised,[14] and many of them want to be gentler and less punitive.[15] *Gentle parenting*, a term coined by British author Sarah Ockwell-Smith, has been a reaction against authoritarian parenting and advocates processing feeling and cultivating empathy.[16] Although some would disagree, I would characterize this approach as low expectations and high support. Based on her experience as an undergraduate psychology student and as a parent, her approach of avoiding disciplining kids has become wildly popular through social media. In my experience, most of the gentle parenting advocates I know also seem to be safetyism proponents.

In a reaction against gentle parenting, some parents are advocating

FAFO (pronounced "faff-oh"), which is short for "F— Around and Find Out." Parents can warn, make rules, or give advice, but if kids do not listen, then they suffer the consequences.[17] FAFO parenting appears to be neither high support nor high expectations—just, "You will figure it out." FAFO parenting advocates are certainly not pushing safetyism. Their kids could achieve some level of status, but they are likely taking risks that are not strategic or safe.

Another type is neglectful or apathetic parenting, which involves low expectations and low support. Kids are free to do anything they want in the real or virtual world, as long as they do not disrupt their parents' work, phone use, or social-media time. While this kind of parenting does not value safetyism, it is catastrophic for developing status or healthy relationships that will lead to resilience.

JOYFUL PARENTS

As kids get older, the parenting challenges change. In a world where the approval of a thirteen-year-old is more valuable than gold, middle-school kids who are seeking status are going to attempt any number of risky behaviors. To an adult, these behaviors might appear to be a deficiency in the brain.

Am I going to jump off the roof into a pool? Should I take my bike off that ramp? Should I post this picture of myself?

What they choose to wear, eat, do, and stream, as well as whom they choose to hang out with, is fraught with complexity. As they move into abstract thinking, they awaken to a world where every interaction has six different frames, which parents also experience.[18]

Listen to this interaction between a mom and a fifteen-year-old son that, at first glance, seems unrelated to status:

Mom: "Take the headset off, stop playing that video game, and take out the trash."

(Mom repeats herself twice; son did not hear due to headset.)

Son: "I will in a minute."

As parents, we know that, in teenager time, this could mean anywhere from sixty seconds to sixty days.

Here is the interaction in six frames:

1. Mom's view of herself: I am a reasonable parent and tired of doing everything around here.
2. Mom's view of her son: I love you, but all you do is rot your brain on video games.
3. Mom's impression of how her son views her: He thinks all I do is nag and takes everything I do for granted.
4. Son's view of himself: I am just hanging out with my friends, and I might have a career in esports. This is career development.
5. Son's view of his mom: Mom is always on me. I can never do anything right, and she has no idea what it is like to be a kid.
6. Son's impression of how his mom views him: Mom thinks I am lazy, waste my time, and pick bad friends.

Does any of this sound familiar?

Parenting is infinitely complex. Imagine how hard this kind of interaction is for kids who have testosterone pumping through their bodies, telling them they need to gain status in an adult world. This means reading what peers and adults think of them, which gets really complicated when every interaction has multiple frames.

Combine that with the complexity of doing this in a virtual world of snaps, texts, and posts that are devoid of physical human contact and, often, context.

What if we could invite kids into a better way to live?

What if parenting could be joyful?

As we've said before, joy flows through adversity, belonging, and curiosity. We need our kids to know that life will be hard, they will always matter to us, and we are curious about them. All of this is grounded in love for them and gritty optimism that they can become more.

Joyful parenting means telling kids who we see them becoming. Young people spend too much time on their curated, virtual personas, and sometimes we as parents spend too much time trying to force kids into molds of who we want them to be (perhaps even who we wish we would have been). The most joyful way to parent is to give kids the opportunity to see their value through our eyes—as whole human beings who have innate worth. It is natural for them to see themselves through the eyes of others, and when we are joyful parents, they can look into our eyes and see delight reflected back at them. They can attain status with us for who they are, not how they perform, and know that they will not gain or lose our love based on their performance.

Our invitation to a better way to live ought to be more than authority-driven compliance. "Because I said so" has never been a good way to get kids to do anything, and it is really problematic when our kids are seeking status. Using any kind of parental trump card that says, "I have status over you, and you will do what I say" diminishes kids at the very time when they are seeking to have status.

How can we approach the video game/trash interaction with status-seeking in mind?

The mom might tell the son (when he is not playing video games), "You're an important team player in this family, and every time you do a chore, you help make our home a better place. Can I count on you to take out the trash every week and help with the dishes after dinner? That would make a big difference."

The son, hearing that he is valued and has status, *might* be more inclined to respond, "Okay."

Later, when he is playing video games instead of doing chores, the mom might remind him that he is needed as a valued member of the family.

An important side note in closing here: I do not recommend paying teenagers for doing chores. This reduces motivation (e.g., when you pay them the first time, it will be expected every time after) and erodes status. If adults in the home do not receive pay for doing work around the house, then paying a kid indicates they have a different status.

MORE WAYS TO SUPPORT STATUS-SEEKING

These past few examples were based on daily interactions with kids that help them develop status as they mature. Those interactions are more important than almost anything else we do as parents, because they are consistent reminders to kids about how we see them.

One of the most fun parts of parenting, however, is getting to be a kid again as we seek adventures with our kids. Certainly, going to exotic places, hiking mountains, sailing, or creating roller coaster memories are amazing ways to help our kids achieve status as adventure seekers. When my kids were nine, I took each one of them for a weekend into Chicago, which was only twenty-five miles away, but it was a different world for them. We took the train, stayed overnight, and just experienced the city. All three still have the posters we made from pictures we took all over the city.

There are many ways to seek adventure without a lot of money. We can invite our kids to head into the woods with us, climb on the roof to watch a sunset, learn how to swim, ride bikes together, go fishing, play football, or change a car battery (the extent of my mechanical skills).

Another way to support status-seeking is celebrating rites of passage for our kids. Jewish culture does this for girls when they turn twelve and boys when they turn thirteen. At that point, they are considered full participants in the community. Latinos celebrate kids entering adulthood when they turn fifteen. The bat mitzva, bar mitzvah, quinceañera, and quinceañero all come with significant costs attached to them, but do they have to?

Parents are picking a year in kids' lives and gathering a community of adults to speak truth into their lives. A family invited me to be a part of this for their son, Jack,[19] when he turned thirteen. The parents asked me and six other men who knew Jack well to share how we had seen him grow and who we saw him becoming. We did this in front of Jack's friends and family. I am sure this felt risky to Jack, but this was a remarkable gift to all of us involved.

There was some food involved in the event, so there was some cost, but I cannot remember the food. What I remember is watching Jack grow in stature as adults spoke truth and love into his life. He didn't have to brag about the biggest roller coaster he had ever ridden. Adults had conferred status on him based on who he was becoming as a man.

An even simpler, lower-cost option? Parents can collect letters from adults who have poured into their kids' lives and give them the letters at a given age.

Investing in the next generation is hard, and each kid is different. One size never fits all, there is no formula, and I am always wary of parenting/teaching/coaching how-to books. I know from experience that coming alongside young people is a lot more fun than punitive, gentle, FAFO, and apathetic approaches.

How could we tap into adversity, belonging, and curiosity? What is a rite of passage we could develop? What is something that could feel strategically adventurous, particularly for those of us who are risk-averse?

In the next chapter, we will explore how we can extend a hospitable welcome to more joyful living.

TAKEAWAY

Safetyism is not the answer for a healthy next generation. We should celebrate kids' strategic risks. Moving away from the idea that "kids do stupid things" to the understanding that "kids do stupid things to gain status" can help us point them to more joy.

TRY THIS

Start small and work your way up!

1. Find a few young people who have taken a strategic social, physical, intellectual, or emotional risk and tell them how you appreciated what they did. (Be careful about public praise, since adult attention can diminish status for middle- and high-school kids.)
2. Let a few kids plan an adventure. This could be a mini adventure like a hike in the woods, a long bike ride, or a game where they make the rules. Or this could be a much larger adventure that takes you all to a new city or country—but give them some autonomy within parameters so they can do some of the planning. Then celebrate the growth that comes through success or failure.

3. Plan a rite of passage with young people. What would help them gain status for who they are becoming in the eyes of their peers or the adults whose opinions they value? Would this involve words of affirmation, a trip, or a challenge? One requirement: Be sure to have fun!

12
HOSPITALITY MEANS KIDS MATTER

Think of your favorite restaurant. What makes it a favorite? I am assuming the food is good. What else makes it a favorite—nostalgia, the environment, the way people make you feel? A good restaurant invites you into an experience. The staff meets a basic need with food and meets a deeper need for connection.

World-famous hospitality expert Will Guidara wrote, "Service is black and white. Hospitality is color."[1] Guidara's leadership of the best restaurant in the world inspired the TV show *The Bear*. In one episode, the owner of "The Bear" described the magic of restaurants and the sense of belonging they create. He said, "At a restaurant, you are never alone."

How do we ensure that kids never feel alone?

Part of the answer lies in a broader understanding of what hospitality is. *Merriam-Webster* defines it as being "readily receptive," giving a "generous and friendly welcome," and "offering a pleasant or sustaining environment."[2] Building on Guidara's belief, I think hospitality is an act of optimism that moves beyond mere service. While service stops at including others, hospitality invites each person to belong.

Sadly, a research study we conducted at the BCSL based on a

representative sample of twenty-four-to-thirty-nine-year-old U.S. high-school graduates showed that less than half felt like they belonged at their high school. This is devastating to me.

Being excluded is tragic.

Being tolerated is better.

Being included is better still.

Belonging is what each heart longs for.[3] It means we matter and others matter to us.[4] It means we are missed when we are not there.

Hospitality is both a cause and an effect of belonging, and it is a key part of experiencing joy through living for and with others.

It is our job as adults to foster a sense of belonging and mattering in kids. More than something that we perform dutifully, humans find great joy through hospitality because it communicates belonging in a way that shows others that they matter. While hospitality will always require work, it is the life-giving work that comes from abundant joy. Life-giving hospitality is sometimes the remedy for exhaustion.

As adults, we need to model life-giving hospitality. When kids know that they matter to others, they will be more joyful and more likely to let others know that they matter to them. And when they do, they will not only be fueled by joy but also experience more joy.

To learn how we adults can cultivate this sense of belonging and mattering, we will explore the role of food, how to live hospitably beyond a remedial middle-school math classroom, and how schools and families demonstrate hospitality on the other side of the world.

FOOD AS HOSPITALITY

Sharing food is an ancient practice of hospitality. We should never take for granted what goes on around the table.

Growing up, my parents sometimes had to get creative to find enough food, even taking my brothers and me behind grocery stores to dumpster-dive for food that was out-of-date but still "good." They certainly were not alone, and even today food insecurity affects forty-seven million people in the United States.[5] When something is scarce, we tend to value it more highly, so it is no surprise that I now see food as an essential vehicle for hospitality.

Here's how it looks in our home.

My family and I make it a habit to eat dinner together and to welcome anyone our kids bring home, because we always have plenty of food. A well-stocked pantry and refrigerator communicate security to me. Welcoming others to share in that food represents abundance.

I am responsible for cooking on the weekends. My wife is a far better cook, but I make four meals reasonably well: hamburgers and hash-brown casserole, chicken quesadillas, poppyseed chicken, and baked ziti or some combination of meat, pasta, cheese, and sauce. This is one of the many ways I show my family they matter to me.

We also host college students for lunch every Sunday during the school year. This tradition began when our son invited fifteen to twenty Baylor students to a meal with us when he was a freshman—that was five years ago. The number of guests has since doubled.

These meals have become an all-hands-on-deck affair as my wife and I hustle to get things ready after church and our youngest daughter makes dessert (her pound cake with strawberries and ice cream melts in the mouth).

We always offer a simple menu, but college kids love free food and being in a home off campus. The invitation remains open to any student who would like a meal in a space with a kitchen table, couches, a backyard, and two dogs.

My wife and I spend more money on that meal each week than our weekly grocery bill because we see it as an investment in people who matter. It is not some kind of performance to boost our image as good, kind people. We do this out of a sense of abundance that is the overflow of the blessings we have experienced.

Our family is certain that we have been more blessed by these Sunday lunches than the students have been. They are our community; we feel like we belong at Baylor more because they belong in our home. Hospitality is a mutually beneficial experience. Welcome breeds welcome. Even before we started hosting Sunday lunches, for over a decade prior we had students over for meals and game nights. Those students were role models for our younger kids, who sometimes would listen to a college student when they could not hear a parent.

When is the last time you invited guests to your table in a way that shows they matter to you?

It doesn't have to be a huge crowd; hosting one or two kids can be even more meaningful. If you can't cook, order takeout. And if you don't want to involve food, gather around another activity.

When you take the initiative to invite young people into your space, you create an opportunity for others to belong and for you to belong. This is one way we make sure kids don't feel alone and support them in learning how to live well with one another by showing others that they matter.

HOSPITABLE LIVING

Hospitality can take many forms, and the next one we will look at involves an example of extreme hospitality. It is not a typical experience or even something I recommend teachers imitate exactly. I include it here because it depicts how hospitality can be a mutual blessing. This story is less about a teacher instructing a student and more about an adult pouring into the life of a kid, and these stories are everywhere. This one just happens to begin in a remedial math classroom.

Remedial math is where students who "hate math" or are "not good at math" go to allow math to die, so the level of student pushback and pessimism is high. It is not the first setting that would come to mind as a hospitable place. The teacher, Mrs. Wiley,[6] worked hard to help students grow their math skills but was more likely to hear students declare to her and the class things like, "I am not taking your bum-ass notes!"

Pushing through the middle-school bluster of students who act like they do not care about years of mathematical failure is a daily requirement for a teacher whose primary goal is to get them to pass a state math test for the first time in years. Like any good teacher, Mrs. Wiley didn't let students' negativity detract her from trying to connect with each of them. She was determined to make her classroom a hospitable invitation to math and, more importantly, to life together.

Emma[7] was one student in great need of a hospitable welcome. She had a 504 plan (a legal document to ensure students with learning differences get what they need from a school) for ADHD and dyslexia. Her mother was an alcoholic, and her dad was in prison for dealing drugs. Despite her challenges, she shared a similar sense of humor with Mrs. Wiley, and they began to connect during lunch or advisory times, when they discussed everything from friends to self-advocacy.

Looking for small ways to help, Mrs. Wiley brought Emma lunch, helped with truancy requirements, and took her backpack home to wash, because other kids were making fun of how bad it smelled.

While the relationship deepened, so did the challenges Emma faced.

In the spring, Emma was hospitalized after overdosing on

medications she found in her mom's bathroom. Mrs. Wiley became the primary point of contact at school, and with the school counselor's approval and encouragement, they developed a safety plan and scheduled formal check-ins to manage stress.

When the year ended, Mrs. Wiley met with Emma's mom to get permission to continue to mentor Emma. With her consent, they ran errands and walked the dog. When the new school year started, Mrs. Wiley picked up Emma on Wednesday nights for dinner, a check-in, homework help, and hanging out. Emma started spending the night so that Mrs. Wiley could drop her off early Thursday morning for tutoring, with a lunch and snacks packed.

Eventually, Emma passed the state math assessment for the first time.

Emma continues to come over on Wednesday nights and is working with Mrs. Wiley to get her driving permit and her first official job. Emma's goal is to become a radiologist technician.

Mrs. Wiley and her husband communicated that Emma matters to them. In return, Emma has reciprocated in ways that let them know they matter to her. Whether it is a pantry and refrigerator filled with Emma's favorite drinks and food, or watching entire seasons of Netflix shows together, Emma knows she matters. Mrs. Wiley knows beyond any doubt that she matters to Emma.

Hospitality is an invitation to mattering. We do not need to do what Mrs. Wiley did to let a kid know that they matter to us. Please do not read about her example and throw up your hands, saying, "Another superhero teacher saves a kid by investing more time and energy than I could ever have."

First, Mrs. Wiley is not a superhero, and in most school contexts, without the direction of a school counselor, this would not even be advisable.

Second, we only need to keep our eyes open for the needs around us to start being hospitable. Greeting a kid by name, remembering to follow up on something that was a concern from a previous conversation, or sitting next to a kid who is sad might be all that is needed to help change the trajectory of a day.

Third, when we begin to change the trajectories of days, we start to change the trajectories of lives. A key to not burning out is finding what is life-giving in the way we carry burdens with others. We just have to be better than a chatbot.

Based on the bleak statistics on loneliness and isolation I listed in chapter 1, we know mattering to others is more important than ever. Young people might be turning to chatbots to feel like they matter to something, but chatbots are not real, cannot give a hug, and will not show up at the hospital when someone is injured. Chatbots can follow algorithms, they can affirm, and they can tell us what is probable. But kids need to know what is possible. More importantly, they need to know they are loved—and they will know they are loved when they know that they matter.

Let them know that today. Look especially for kids who are marginalized. They will be on the edges of groups, quietly waiting for someone to notice them, hoping someone will offer a little kindness, wondering if anyone misses them when they are not there. They need to know that you do.

When was the last time you told a kid that you missed them?

SCHOOL HOSPITALITY

I've never seen an entire school that shows kids they matter quite like one place in Australia. Walking onto the pre-K–12 school campus, my seventeen-year-old daughter and I were surrounded by students ranging in age from four to eighteen. Some students were sitting or standing in a courtyard beside a tree-lined pond. Others were walking into a glass-walled building that created a seamless transition from indoor to outdoor. Inside the building was the "Breakfast Club," a place where students could grab something for breakfast and sit around café tables. There was a thirty-five-meter Ferris wheel being erected on the oval[8] for a weekend fete[9] that would welcome thousands of community members. Moms walked upstairs to join a yoga group led by a teacher at the school.

Parents come to the student-run café on campus every day. The school is a community hub. The welcome is intentional and casual. The best word to describe the school climate is *delightful*.

The hospitable welcome was intentional and a response to student needs. A few years ago a teacher noticed that some students were coming to school hungry, so she started the Breakfast Club. She brought in a few toasters and went to a local bakery at the end of each day to get bread they had not sold. The following day, she would provide hundreds of pieces of toast to hungry kids. Toast became a hospitable welcome to learning without a protesting stomach. Today, the Breakfast Club is staffed by two teachers and six to eight students every day and is now part of the culture of the school.

While U.S. schools have to operate differently due to safety considerations, there are several things we can learn from this type of organization-wide hospitality. First, at this Australian school, every person who walks on campus feels like they belong. Administrators and teachers greet everyone, and because it is a community hub, the school feels like an intergenerational resource. Other Australian school leaders purposely built their school near a retirement community so that the students and older adults could be mutually beneficial. Could we find ways to bring more generations into schools?

Second, at the Australian campus, due to the year-round temperate climate, there is little separation between indoor and outdoor spaces. Adults and students move freely between them, which grounds everything in nature. Could we find ways to create more outdoor spaces for learning?

Third, food and drink are central to the Australian school's hospitality. The school team greet adults with coffee,[10] and morning tea await every student and adult a few hours later—a time when students could get a drink or a small snack and have time to socialize outdoors. I am all for adding tea to our U.S. school mornings!

Our final example of hospitality also comes from the other side of the world, this one involving a family and two unlikely components: rugby and grief.

HOSPITALITY AND RUGBY

I do not know much about rugby other than it looks like football without helmets, but a family rugby team called "The Rising Sons" made me want to learn more. By their own admission, they are not very good, but this team is about far more than winning.

They play in a seven-on-seven league and an annual rugby tournament. Sixty-year-old Ian Liney, a huge fan of the world-famous New Zealand All Blacks, leads the crew of his brothers, sons, and nephews.

If competitiveness is a gene, then it is a genetic trait of the Lineys. Everything is a competition, whether it is getting to the top of a snow-capped New Zealand mountain, hiking through the Australian bush, or jumping into an ice-covered lake wearing only budgie smugglers.[11] The family exuberantly roasts one another about physical endeavors that did not pan out well or were not performed with alacrity.

Tackling hard things is what brings the family together. Several years ago, one of Ian's brothers died in a tragic motorcycle accident, when a high driver hit him with a car. Ian's three nephews lost their father, but they continue to play rugby with the people who remember and love their dad as well.

Even grieving can be a form of hospitality. Life is hard, and none of us escapes suffering, loss, or trauma. Stephen Colbert lost his father and two of his brothers when he was ten years old, and in reflection has said, "It is a gift to exist, and with existence comes suffering. There is no escaping that."[12]

Life is a gift. In life, we will suffer. How can we help our kids understand this and find joy?

Part of it involves showing them that we only get through life with others. There is a time to process grief and sit with loss. Sometimes we process with words, but grieving with others always requires presence, even presence in the form of a family rugby team. Our presence can be a hospitable invitation to life—life with and beyond grief.

Over time, we might find ways to remember and celebrate the ones we've lost by doing the things they loved with the people they loved. For some families, like the Lineys, that might be competition, teasing, and relentless good-natured trash talk. Whatever form it takes, it is a generously hospitable invitation to life together.

If we want to build a generation that will know they matter, hospitality is the way. We do not just serve others as adults. We welcome them into life-giving relationships in the way we invite them to our tables, rugby teams, campuses, and homes. The key is just to get started and celebrate progress. Joy is not a destination—which is why the final chapter in this book is devoted to the joy we can find in progress.

TAKEAWAY

Hospitality communicates that kids matter to us, and we matter to them. Service can feel like an obligation, but hospitality is an opportunity to extend and experience belonging.

TRY THIS

Again, start small, and remember it is not hospitality if it feels like a chore.

What do you enjoy doing that could become a hospitable welcome to kids? Do you enjoy fishing, running, cooking, or reading? What could you invite kids into? What is something the young people in your life do that they might welcome your involvement in?

One of my daughters once wrote on a card that she really appreciated that I "am interested in the things that she is interested in." Certainly, there are many things that I am not interested in that a twenty-year-old might be, but finding areas of overlapping interest and encouragement is hospitable.

If you are up for advanced hospitality, who in your life is grieving or suffering in some other way and just needs your presence? This might be the most hospitable thing you can do, and there might be joy on the other side of the grieving or suffering.

13
CHASE PROGRESS, NOT SUCCESS

"We just want our kids to be happy."

"We just want our kids to be safe."

"We just want our kids to be successful."

Now that we've reached the final chapter, it's time to examine this third statement of parental wants. Of happiness, safety, and success, success might be the hardest to define.

My greatest joys in working with kids have come from the progress we have made together. The summit of success might be the goal, but the climb is often where the joy is. I have already shared the story of Amanda, who passed away when she was sixteen from catastrophic epilepsy. Was that success?

What about the family rugby team in New Zealand that, by their own admission, is not very good? Is that success?

How about the baker who served in WWII and stopped attending school when he was twelve? Was that success?

Consider how you view success using these questions about different age groups and the experience of supporting them.

1. What is success for ten-year-olds? Are they "popular," on a travel team, well-dressed, and use deodorant? Or are they kind, curious, and willing to do hard things?
2. What is success for sixteen-year-olds? Are they past pubescent awkwardness, attractive, high achieving, and living a well-curated life online? Or are they good at letting others know they matter? Are they passionate? Are they compassionate?
3. What is success for twenty-two-year-olds? Are they college graduates with well-paying jobs? Are they social-media influencers in their parents' basements? Or are they well-adjusted, thoughtful young adults who are becoming more of who they are meant to be as they develop identity capital?
4. What is success for parents? Do you define your success by what others think of your kids, how they behave, and what they accomplish? Are your kids primarily extensions of yourself that either build or erode your self-worth? Or are your kids learning from your example that there can be joy through adversity because identity is not based on performance?

Messy exercise, right? I particularly struggle with these as a parent and educator. We all say that we value the holistic development of the young people whom we support, but often the success score card has limited criteria. I do not want to derive my self-worth from my kids or students, but I often fall into this trap. I do not want education to just be about economic success, but I do want my kids to be gainfully employed.

Is success something that is achieved?

Is success a mountain kids conquer for themselves, or is it a mountain that conquers kids (shaping them for the better) when they realize that life is better when lived for others?[1]

Maybe we are more likely to find joy on the way up the mountain.

Have you ever had the experience of chasing something you thought would bring ultimate happiness, but when you got it, it didn't make you happy? The same is going to be true for today's kids.

Measuring success by measuring happiness is problematic. First, as we have established, happiness is circumstantial. Second, happiness as a goal is a problem, because when we set a goal, we have to measure progress toward that goal. As we measure progress, we will regularly find we have not met the level of happiness we aspire to. This awareness that our happiness is lacking then erodes our sense of well-being because we are always seeing ourselves as operating at a deficit.[2]

Take any big task that you attempt. This could be a corporate deal, a piece of art, the development of your own body, or a big event. Consider the process an author goes through to write a book. Shouldn't holding the book in your hands when it is completed be the happiest moment of the entire experience? Similarly, shouldn't closing the deal, finishing the piece of art, achieving a fit body, or hosting a successful event be the happiest moment? For me, that has not been true.

That is not even true for this book. Finishing writing is not the most joyful (note, I have shifted from "happy" to "joyful") part of the process. The best part is improving the book with others in the revision process. The book in my mind is always better than the final product.[3] No matter how good the final product, the abstract ideal in my mind will always be just out of reach, so I have to enjoy the journey toward the goal I will never fully realize.

The same is likely true for making deals, creating art, working out, and creating a big event.

When we focus on progress, we can experience joy because we were built to create.

REJECTING ACCOMPLISHMENT-CONTINGENT SELF-WORTH

As we celebrate progress, we still have to be careful not to tie our human value to it. Dr. Elizabeth Bounds, a former two-sport college athlete and a researcher who studies sports, used the phrase "accomplishment-contingent self-worth" to refer to this issue.[4] Haven't we all had times when we thought our value as humans was dependent on what we could achieve? I felt it every time I stepped on a basketball or tennis court. Pathetically, I still sometimes feel it when I step on a pickleball court.

Here is what this might sound like from kids' perspectives as it relates to their parents, educators, and coaches:

1. "You are so smart. You got all A's. We love you so much!"
2. "What is wrong with you? You are better than B's and C's."
3. "You are the best player on your team. I don't know why the coach doesn't see how valuable you are."

Here is what kids might take away:

1. My value is dependent on being a good student. Intelligence is a trait.
2. My value is connected to my grades, and my parent thinks I fall short.
3. My value is dependent on how I play.

Our kids have to know that their value is not contingent on their performance. If success is our goal for them, they can get crushed under the weight of our expectations. With idealized images of themselves seared into their minds, dreams can turn into disappointment. Certainly, some kids will make it to the NBA, but probably not the kid who tops out his height at five feet, five inches. Even for those who do, attaining what they perceive as success, happiness, and security often does not stick. Over half of NBA and NFL players end up broke within five years of leaving their respective leagues.[5] Even for those who achieve financial success, many find the success to be hollow.

Part of the problem lies with how we define *success*, which we addressed at the beginning of this chapter. I asked an accomplished professor in his seventies what success looked like for raising his own kids. He said, "I want them to be decent people."

That seems reasonable, but what does "decent" mean, and is that really the ultimate goal?

Other parents tell me that success is happiness. "I just want my kids to do what makes them happy."

When I ask, "Do you do what makes you happy?" most acknowledge that this has not been their lot in life, but they still hope that for their kids.

Some of us can live in a bubble, thinking that if we can just get our kids on the right teams, in the right schools, with the right connections, success is sure to follow. For many kids, however, that is like jumping on a treadmill that is constantly accelerating its speed. They run as fast as they can, but they do not sense their progress or know when they arrive at success.

Sadly, many of us model this for kids. How much is enough? When do we stop trying to prove ourselves? If we cannot get this right as adults, how can we expect kids to find their way?

Since we have established that adults and kids alike struggle to define *happiness*, *safety*, and *success*, we know that we will not experience joy on the backside of those ill-defined goals. Wouldn't it be much easier to identify progress along the way?

Isn't that where joy is, anyway?

RECORDING PROGRESS

As I was writing this book, my youngest daughter began her senior year in high school, so she had her "last first day" of her K-12 school years. As a dad, I was a little sad because I love first days of school. I have experienced forty-five first days of school—the beauty of being an educator. Those first days represent the chance to begin again.

I track progress in school years for my own kids as well as for my students. The night before the last day of school is always a tough one for me. Invariably, my hand is cramping, and my eyes are starting to blur around 2:00 a.m. Employing a practice that many teachers have used for years, I write to each of my students. When I first started teaching, these were handwritten letters to tell each student how I had seen them grow, who they were becoming, and what I was hoping for them as they moved to middle school. Now I teach undergraduate and graduate students, so I write inscriptions in books to offer encouragement.

Writing these notes is a way for me to wring out the final drops of joy from a year filled with triumph and struggle. When teachers and students separate annually, the relationship does not end, but it changes. The collective identity of a fifth-grade or doctoral-level class shifts. This shift causes a bittersweet melancholy to well up in me. While closure is never complete, these written reminders are my way of acknowledging how our struggles have led to joy.

My joy as a teacher is found in the growth observed in my students. While the work can be exhausting, it is always life-giving when we see and celebrate progress.

As a dad, as soon as we knew we were going to have a child, I started a journal. Then I got a new journal for each child that followed. In each journal, I recorded how I saw each kid growing, the funny things they did, and what I was praying for them. I find great joy in looking back over old entries to see how they have changed and how they have not. I can celebrate the progress that the journals mark.

In fact, the only way to celebrate progress is to mark it.

I will always pray for my kids, but the struggle for me has been to know when to give them the journals. When are the journals "complete"? Do I just let them find them when they clean out the house when I am dead? Selfishly, I did not want that because we wouldn't be able to talk about the ways they have grown based on the anecdotes that I recorded.

This past summer, my son, Ben, married an incredible woman. As the wedding approached, I felt like maybe this was the time. At the rehearsal dinner, I spoke for a few minutes, reading from the journal aloud to share my first prayers for him and for his wife. When I finished, I handed him the journal and told him that I would continue to pray for him, but that the journal was his. He could see himself through my eyes as a new dad and know how loved he had been since before he was born.

Giving him the journal was hard. Selfishly, I was handing over two decades of writing about my firstborn child. Would he think it was cheesy? Would he find value in it? Would he judge me for the months-long gaps when I did not write anything? Would he even keep track of it in the swirl of the wedding?

A couple of weeks after the wedding, Ben sent me a text that read, "I finished your journal last night and was a bit of an emotional wreck. It is the greatest gift I have ever been given. Talk more this weekend."

Ben is far from a finished product, but there is so much joy in celebrating the progress he has made through his literal first steps to his figurative first steps as an adult. Allowing him to observe his progress and my love reflected back to him through the pages of a journal was a gift to him. His response was a gift to me.

I have many failings as a father, and I share this here only to demonstrate how much joy there is in recording progress. This is not a prescription; I am by no means recommending you write notes or keep a journal for kids like I did. Part of what I do for a living is writing, so this approach felt natural to me. If you are a verbal processor, make it a habit to tell kids how you see them growing. If you are less likely to use words, then give the gift of your presence. Sometimes a smile or a hug from someone who uses words judiciously is more meaningful than a journal full of words from someone like me.

CELEBRATE YOUR KIDS' PROGRESS

Let's explore more ways you can do this with the young people in your life. How are the kids in your classrooms, fields, and homes better today than they were yesterday? Think about them holistically. This is not just another way to measure incremental success. Moving from measuring success forty years into the future to forty minutes into the future at the end of a workout or study session is just another way of living life on a treadmill. We can celebrate who they are becoming and speak truth into their lives by telling them where we see progress.

Consider what Norwegians do with their kids in athletics. They have created one of the best sports development systems in the world. In the 2026 Milan/Cortina Winter Games, Norway, a country of 5.6 million people, won eighteen gold medals and forty-one medals overall, by far the most of any country. How? Through joy. Their national youth sports strategy is "Joy of Sport for All." Kids do not specialize in a sport at a young age, and sports are about having fun with family and friends. What if we, as parents and coaches, followed their lead and lived "a single principle underlying why they turn up each week, underpinning every conversation with a child entrusted to them: to create an experience of joy."[6] The goal is not to build the next Johannes *Høsflot Klæbo*, who has won eleven gold medals in one of the most grueling sports ever—cross-country skiing—by telling kids to suffer; instead, we are to allow joy to emerge for each kid and then see what they can become.

It can be helpful to go back to the ABCs—adversity, belonging, and curiosity.

ADVERSITY

How have our kids leaned into adversity by doing something hard, something they couldn't do a month ago?

Did they have a hard conversation with a friend? Did they speak up for someone who was being bullied? Did they write papers on their own without off-loading the hard mental work to AI? Did they see a need in the house and handle it without being asked, like an overflowing garbage can that made it out to the curb? Did they show up for someone who was hurting? Did they ask a hard question about why we exist as humans?

If you can answer yes to any of these questions, go celebrate that with your kid! Tell them you see them. You are grateful for them. We are not celebrating mediocrity with trophies for all. We are celebrating who they are becoming. This is also not celebrating kids for expected tasks like turning in homework, doing the dishes, or showing up to practice. We are speaking life into how we see them becoming who they are meant to be.

Write down as many questions as you can that will help you comprehensively think about the kids you serve and how they might be leaning into adversity. Think about all of these different types of adversity: mental, relational, physical, spiritual, and emotional. List as many as you can.

If you know kids who are making progress in any of these areas, send them a text, write them a note, or best of all, look them in the eye and give words to the progress you see them making. They need to hear this. So often, they lose sight of how they are growing because it is hard to see from *A* to *B*. Sometimes it is easier to see the growth by looking a few more steps down the road—maybe seeing from *A* to *L* rather than just from *A* to *B*.

Best of all, these questions will help them tell their own stories. Those stories build the muscles we need around our backbones. Those stories are joy.

BELONGING

How have the kids you serve shown you that you matter? How have they shown others that their teammates, peers, and others in their community matter? What tangible things have they done that communicate that others matter?

Kids show up for each other in remarkable ways. Keep your eyes open, and you will see this all around you. One of our daughters had been sick for a week with a 103.7 degree fever. A friend showed up with flowers and a basket of some of her favorite treats, from candy to carrots. The same daughter broke up with a long-term boyfriend later that same week. I watched another friend show up at 10:00 p.m. with Ben & Jerry's and a minutes-long embrace as they cried together.

From middle-school basketball teams who show up for a teammate who is struggling in a drill to college students who provide family support for kids who are far from home, kids show one another they matter every day. If you want to be encouraged, just keep looking for the ways they demonstrate how much they matter to one another. At Baylor, I see humans loving other humans in the way they walk together, build floats for homecoming, and share clothing and food with those who do not have as much. For most students—although I am sure there are some unfortunate exceptions—there seems to be a sense that we are all doing life together. As a middle-school teacher, I saw it in the kids who reached out to the kids who sat alone at lunch, welcomed kids into lab groups, or let others know that they were missed.

Communicating that kids matter is a great way to celebrate progress. This happens in two ways. First, kids feel like they are growing when they feel more like they belong. The growth is no longer just about the individual. Individuals might be able to be well on their own, but they flourish when they matter to others. Second, modeling how kids matter to us helps them see how to communicate to others that they matter. When we celebrate the ways they help others feel like they belong, we make progress as groups and communities. We can all feel it.

CURIOSITY

Finally, look for progress in how kids communicate curiosity. Of the three ABCs, this is the one that seems to diminish the most through formal education. For most kids, school diminishes academic curiosity. As a society, we also seem to be less curious about others. If truth is the source of curiosity, how can we cultivate more seekers of truth?

Again, take some time to write down some questions. Since we are talking about curiosity, this list will likely correlate with your general disposition toward curiosity. Are you most joyful when you know you are right? Are you most joyful when you are seeking others' stories?

How can we teach our kids to be curious about the world and others? By being curious about the world and about them!

Fan the flames of their curiosity so they will become increasingly curious. When you read, see, or hear something you disagree with, express curiosity instead of judgment. If you are watching something with kids and someone expresses an opinion or does something that runs counter to your values, ask questions or wonder. Statements like, "I wonder what might have happened to him that made him react that way," or questions like, "What are the possible consequences of a decision like that? Do you know people who make decisions like that? Why do you think they do?" are far more helpful than my typical responses.

My responses sometimes tend toward, "That is so ridiculous. Who would do something like that? He is going to get what he deserves. This is what is wrong with our country." An incurious adult does not help kids become more curious.

Kids should become increasingly curious as they get older. Their curiosity might shift from dinosaurs to the opposite sex, sports, and their purpose in the world, but we should celebrate the questions they ask. Kids quit learning when they stop asking questions.

Poet Rainer Maria Rilke wrote, "Be patient to all that is unsolved in your heart and try to love the questions themselves. . . . Live the questions now. Perhaps you will then gradually, without noticing it, live along some distant day into the answer."[7]

Celebrate the great questions kids ask. Explore the questions with them. Be fearless with them in their pursuit of deeper truth.

TELLING A BETTER STORY

We started this book with Dante's story. I would love to be able to return to his life story and tell you how he progressed after high school. But Dante is gone; his story ended.

Instead, I want to guide you in seeking a story from a kid you love. We explored this in chapter 8, but it is worth revisiting here in the context of focusing on progress. Kids need to tell their own stories of how they have found joy through adversity, because knowing and telling those stories build their resilience and joy.

Here is a simple story frame. Try it yourself, then pick a few kids to try it too. Choose the questions that are right for their age and see what they come up with.

1. **When did you do something you initially doubted you could do?**

   Possible ideas:

   » learn to bike, swim, read, or write an essay

   » befriend someone who was unkind

   » break up with a boyfriend or girlfriend

   » complete a long hike

   » survive an illness

   » overcome an injury

   » help a friend who did not want to be helped at first

   » work with a team to reach a seemingly insurmountable goal

   » answer the question of why you exist

   » show up for a friend

- » endure the loss of a loved one
- » speak in front of others
- » stick up for yourself
- » love someone who disappointed you
- » recognize that you were not going to reach a goal and would need to pivot
- » realize that your identity is not in your performance

2. **Why did you think it would be hard?**

   Be honest. This is the time to describe all the reasons why things looked bleak. Do not rush through this part. Consider:

   - » What was the source of your self-doubt?
   - » What caused you to doubt?
   - » Were the beliefs well-founded?
   - » Did others also think that you could not do the thing?
   - » What evidence did you have that you could not do it?

3. **What happened that surprised you? What was the breakthrough?**

   At some point in every story of resilience, there is a breakthrough moment that surprises us.

   - » Who showed up?
   - » What skill developed?
   - » What work paid off?
   - » How did the team work together?

4. **How are you different now than you were before?**
   » What are you more capable of now than you were before?
   » How have you become more of who you were meant to be?
   » How are the people around you better?
   » What is something else you do not think you can do that you would like to try?
   » Who else can you invite to join you?

5. **Where did you see joy emerge?**
   Even if things are not completely resolved and you still struggle with who you are becoming through adversity, consider:
   » Do you feel you belong?
   » Are you more curious?
   » How would you describe your joy?
   » How did others experience joy?

Again, before you ask a kid to do this, go through the five questions yourself. Come up with your own story frame and share it as an example to guide the kid. Your vulnerability will build their trust in you as a listener.

Here is my story frame:

- I never thought I would be a college professor (Question 1).
- As a shy, dyslexic elementary-school kid who eventually graduated from a poor West Virginia high school, I lived most of my

childhood with a scarcity mindset. Being a college professor was not even in the realm of possibility for me (Question 2).

- Because I looked like Appalachian poverty, I got a scholarship to attend college, where I learned to love to teach, read, write, think, and speak to large groups of people (Question 3).
- I moved from a mindset of scarcity to one of abundance after I found that joy was possible through struggle as long as it was alongside others (Question 4).
- Joy emerges daily when I see what young people are capable of doing and see the small contributions I make to parents and leaders helping others become more of who they were meant to be (Question 5).

That five-sentence story might not be that compelling for you as a reader, but that is not the point. The point is for you to find your story so you can help others find their stories. Inspiration for these stories can come from little moments that might be overlooked in the busyness of life and only become evident as markers of transformation down the road. Once we find our story, telling it over and over again (to ourselves and others) fuels joy and builds resilience.

Veterans keep coming to Brad Livingstone's classes to tell their stories to the next generation. By humbly sharing why they served, they help kids understand the price of the freedom they enjoy. When students shake veterans' hands and thank them for their service, there is mutual joy because of the veterans' resilience.

Divine kept showing up to school after being beaten by school leaders and made it to a university in the United States. She allowed me to include her story and her name in this book because she is a powerful force who has seen how cruel the world can be and, with her clear-eyed gritty optimism, will make it better.

Grace, my youngest daughter, who once declared herself a disappointment to everyone including herself, graduated from high school this year and is headed to college. She believes she has inherent worth that is not accomplishment-contingent. Her story is far from fully written, but she no longer questions her self-worth when things get hard. Adversity has led to a maturity that allows joy to emerge through her struggles.

My kids are now twenty-three, twenty, and eighteen years old. I do not know what success will look like for them, and it is not my place to define that success. Based on what I read in the journals I have kept for each of them, I do know they have made a lot of progress toward understanding

- where their hope is (not in themselves),
- where their identity is (not in their performance), and
- how they live their lives (not for themselves).

They can attest that progress often involves suffering, but there is still joy.

In the Christian tradition, another word for *progress* is *sanctification*. In this life, Christians do not believe that we can achieve perfection, but we do believe that God can work in and through us in ways that make us more like Jesus Christ. The process of sanctification is sometimes painful and might require us to endure suffering, but there is joy in the refining process as we realize that life is less about us and more about Christ.

However you want to frame it, humans find the most meaning, connection, and transformation when we embrace that life can be both hard *and* joyful.

So invite kids into this better way of life. Through your own words and actions, acknowledge how your struggles have led to joy. Show kids that "a rich life—a good life—is forged from precisely the things that make it hard."[8] They will notice.

Stop worrying about success. Notice and celebrate progress instead.

Draw stories out of kids that move beyond happiness to them owning how much they have overcome. Encourage them to keep rehearsing those stories, which will steer them away from toxic positivity, reinforce their capacity for growth, and instill gritty optimism in them for all that lies ahead.

Let Disneyland maintain its claim as the "happiest place on earth." We want something better. Let's make our schools and homes the most joyful places on earth—where people work together to embrace adversity, build belonging, and cultivate curiosity.

After all, we don't just want our kids to be happy, safe, or successful.

We want our kids to be joyful.

TAKEAWAY

Success is a moving target at best. Progress is worth the daily chase because there is joy in doing hard things with others.

TRY THIS

Use the five questions to tell your story. Don't overthink it. You read my simple five-sentence story; these are not meant to be literary works of art. Our stories just have to be honest.

Once you have written your story, share it with several young people, and ask them the five questions. See what they can do, or let them go first!

These stories are all works in progress because that is what life is—progress toward something better.

ACKNOWLEDGMENTS

Given all that has been written about happiness, having the audacity to write a book critiquing happiness required the courage and wisdom of a lot of people. I offer this book humbly based on the evidence of joy we have found around the world. Many of the people are named in chapters, others I have kept private, but you will see their influence throughout the book because they have shaped me and shown me a better way to live.

Thanking people in acknowledgments is always hard because I know I will leave people out who have made vital contributions. However, I have to start by acknowledging our team at the Baylor Center for School Leadership, which has helped build a culture of joy in the work we do every day, because that is the basis of the book. Your examples and insights have been invaluable. Erik Ellefsen—this book feels like a lifetime in the making for us. Thanks for being one of my greatest sources of joy. Sahira Kodra—you pursue joy over happiness with everyone you meet and everything you do. Krystle Moos—you are one of the most conscientious and caring people I know. Alison Treadaway—you have so much wisdom as a friend, colleague, and parent. Bill Sterrett—you are an amazing leader and friend.

A book like this requires a wide range of research support. Hannah Kapitaniuk—you have contributed so much to this project and all the work of the last few years with your amazing mind for research, your compassion, and your honest feedback. You have been such a blessing as you have kept me sane *and* laughing. Wendi Singletary—thank you for your deep insights and wisdom based on decades of parenting and outstanding teaching. Meredith Frey—thanks for embodying joy and helping with the podcast. Thanks to all the Baylor graduate students leading schools around the world who provided examples of the joy we find through struggle—you all are tremendous gifts to me and the communities you serve. Turtles for life!

Thanks for wisdom from Chris Allen, Abby Andrietsch, Bill and Christi Bachman, Jake Baskin, Kenny Berry, Andrew and Nina Brenneman, Shaun Brooker, Blair Browning, Matt Burchett, Robert and Lynda Copple, Herb Cox, Christina Crook, Joel and Tracy Eckert, Malinda Golden, Bryan Goodwin, John Hattie, Bobby Ott, Mike Rogers, Tiffany Spicer, Darren Spyksma, and Matt Thomas. Because this book is written to a wide audience, your perspectives as experts in your fields and as parents were invaluable.

Thanks to JP for connecting me to Don Gates and both of them for connecting me to the HarperCollins team. You believed in this book immediately. Having friends like JP, an agent like Don, and an incredible publishing team has been so life-giving. Carrie Marrs—your investment in this book as an editor has been such a gift. From getting feedback from Mads to deeply engaging these ideas as a parent, you made this book so much better.

Finally, I have to thank my family. Because this is a book about joy, you show up on so many pages. Ben, Sarah, and Grace, thank you for all you have taught me, for the way you love our family, and for giving me hope for what God can do through flawed parents who love their kids very much. Carolyn, you have been His greatest gift to me and are the reason I can write a book about joy because of the animating hope we share.

NOTES

PART 1

1. David Yeager argues convincingly that we should consider the age of twenty-five as a good transition point to consider, given how the brain develops. For our purposes, birth to age twenty-five can work as "not yet an adult." David S. Yeager, *10 to 25: A Groundbreaking Approach to Leading the Next Generation—and Making Your Own Life Easier* (Simon & Schuster, 2024).
2. Jonathan Haidt, *The Anxious Generation: How the Great Rewiring of Childhood Is Causing an Epidemic of Mental Illness* (Penguin, 2024).

CHAPTER 1

1. This is a pseudonym.
2. "Data and Statistics on Children's Mental Health," U.S. Centers for Disease Control, updated June 5, 2025, accessed February 9, 2026, https://www.cdc.gov/children-mental-health/data-research/index.html.
3. "Youth Risk Behavior Survey: Data Summary & Trends Report," U.S. Centers for Disease Control, updated 2023, accessed February 9, 2026, https://www.cdc.gov/healthyyouth/data/yrbs/pdf/YRBS_Data-Summary-Trends_Report2023_508.pdf.
4. Zach Rausch and Jonathan Haidt, *The Anxious Generation: The Evidence*, latest data reported runs from 2010 to 2022, updated 2025, accessed February 9, 2026, https://www.anxiousgeneration.com/research/the-evidence.
5. Ibid.

6. https://docs.google.com/spreadsheets/d/1KubvawMZ-AbD1u1zxsjjcBtJZlw39rIjawI-y-8DY-c/edit?gid=0#gid=0.
7. Ibid. "Suicide rates are higher for Gen Z girls in the U.S., U.K., Canada, Australia, and New Zealand than any previous generation when they were young." In 2022, the suicide rate for fifteen- to nineteen-year-old boys was three times higher than that of girls.
8. Due to the lag in reporting data, the most recent year available at the time of writing was 2022. Alison L. Cammack, Mark R. Stevens, Rebecca B. Naumann, Jing Wang, Wojciech Kaczkowski, Jorge Valderrama, et al., "*Vital Signs*: Suicide Rates and Selected County-Level Factors—United States, 2022," U.S. Centers for Disease Control, updated September 19, 2024, accessed February 9, 2026, https://doi.org/10.15585/mmwr.mm7337e1.
9. "Youth Risk Behavior Survey: Data Summary & Trends Report," U.S. Centers for Disease Control, updated 2013–2023, accessed February 9, 2026, https://www.cdc.gov/yrbs/dstr/pdf/YRBS-2023-Data-Summary-Trend-Report.pdf.
10. "Data and Statistics on Children's Mental Health," U.S. Centers for Disease Control, June 25, 2025, https://www.cdc.gov/children-mental-health/data-research/index.html.
11. Olivia Sappenfield, Cinthya Alberto, Jessica Minnaert, Julie Donney, Lydie Lebrun-Harris, and Reem Ghandour, "Adolescent Mental and Behavioral Health, 2023," National Center for Biotechnology Information, National Library of Medicine, October 2024, https://www.ncbi.nlm.nih.gov/books/NBK608531/.
12. "Anxiety Disorders—Facts & Statistics," Anxiety and Depression Association of America, updated October 2025, accessed February 9, 2026, https://adaa.org/understanding-anxiety/facts-statistics.
13. Jorge V. Verlenden, Ari Fodeman, Natalie Wilkins, Sherry Everett Jones, Shamia Moore, et al., "Mental Health and Suicide Risk Among High School Students and Protective Factors—Youth Risk Behavior Survey, United States, 2023," U.S. Centers for Disease Control, updated October 10, 2024, accessed February 9, 2026, https://www.cdc.gov/mmwr/volumes/73/su/su7304a9.htm?utm_source=chatgpt.com.

14. https://docs.google.com/spreadsheets/d/1tdYcnf3ziuMMp8GyPafDNpIWj-lZOf9CmO17Tg_MIZo/edit?gid=879215710#gid=879215710.
15. Michael B. Robb, "The New Normal: Parents, Teens, Screens, and Sleep in the United States," Common Sense Media, updated 2019, accessed February 9, 2026, https://www.commonsensemedia.org/sites/default/files/research/report/2019-new-normal-parents-teens-screens-and-sleep-united-states-report.pdf.
16. Justin Martin, Stephen Song, Chighaf Bakour, Wendy M. Rote, Logan T. Rance, Joshua M. Scacco, et al., *Life in Media Survey: A Baseline Study of Digital Media Use and Well-Being Among 11- to 13-Year-Olds* (University of South Florida, 2025), lifeinmediasurvey.org.
17. Ran Barzilay, Samuel D. Pimentel, Kate T. Tran, Elina Visoki, David Pagliaccio, and Randy P. Auerback, "Smartphone Ownership, Age of Smartphone Acquisition, and Health Outcomes in Early Adolescence," *Pediatrics*, updated December 1, 2025, accessed February 10, 2026, https://doi.org/10.1542/peds.2025-072941.
18. "American Time Use Study—Isolation, Friendship, and Companionship," accessed February 10, 2026, https://docs.google.com/spreadsheets/d/1ZuL25ZBEvBfc0IbWsdtuqw0N0X0SNne6ujZCa7us1Bg/edit?gid=70986005#gid=70986005.
19. Rausch and Haidt, *The Anxious Generation*, Chapter 6: Online Supplement, "Why Social Media Harms Girls More Than Boys," https://docs.google.com/document/d/1IXkCo9SEpuCY_AUeWYPhyRRwWXKw_RupiXgd06sU1Ec/edit?tab=t.0 Additionally, worldwide, one in five teenagers report being lonely according to https://cdn.who.int/media/docs/default-source/who-commission-on-social-connection/whocsc-plainlanguage-en_comp.pdf?sfvrsn=c5396dff_6&download=true.
20. Michael B. Robb and Supreet Mann, "Boys in the Digital Wild: Online Culture, Identity, and Well-Being," Common Sense Media, updated 2025, accessed February 9, 2026, https://www.commonsensemedia.org/sites/default/files/research/report/2025-boys-in-the-digital-wild-report_for-web.pdf.
21. "Our Epidemic of Loneliness and Isolation: The U.S. Surgeon General's Advisory on the Healing Effects of Social Connection and

Community," Office of the U.S. Surgeon General, updated 2023, accessed February 9, 2026, https://www.hhs.gov/sites/default/files/surgeon-general-social-connection-advisory.pdf?.

22. Rausch and Haidt, *The Anxious Generation*, https://docs.google.com/spreadsheets/d/16ldvJkww7Mp6zsP_OPP_WXZ6OZSJEqoTO90YCxt4AvE/edit?gid=202143982#gid=202143982.
23. For example, Candice Odgers, a developmental psychologist, argues that she has failed to find compelling evidence of the damages of digital-technology use in ten- to fifteen-year-olds. Failure to reject the null hypothesis does not mean that there is no effect, but she argues that adult "panic" over smartphones doesn't help teens. She cites her own kids liking "cat attacks dog" videos on TikTok as a fortunate outcome of her wisdom to allow them phones and social media. Candice L. Odgers, "The Panic over Smartphones Doesn't Help Teens," *Atlantic*, updated May 21, 2024, accessed February 9, 2026, https://www.theatlantic.com/technology/archive/2024/05/candice-odgers-teens-smartphones/678433/.
24. This book is intentionally not a work for peer review and directed toward a broad audience. I have prioritized accessibility while citing evidence for this reason.
25. Putnam and Garrett describe how historians look for overarching narratives without being as concerned about causes. Quantitative social scientists will only believe a narrative if a cause can be identified. Conversely, historians become skeptical when a cause is identified because history is more complicated than a simple cause. For our purposes, certainly there are many factors that have affected our kids. Robert D. Putnam with Shaylyn Romney Garrett, *The Upswing: How America Came Together a Century Ago and How We Can Do It Again* (Simon & Schuster, 2020).
26. Julia Moeller, Marc A. Brackett, Zorana Ivcevic, and Arielle E. White, "High School Students' Feelings/Discoveries from a Large National Survey and an Experience Sampling Study," *Learning and Instruction* 66 (April 2020): 101301, https://doi.org/10.1016/j.learninstruc.2019.101301.
27. "E-Cigarette Use Among Youth," U.S. Centers for Disease Control,

updated October 17, 2024, accessed February 9, 2026, https://www.cdc.gov/tobacco/e-cigarettes/youth.html#:~:text=E%2Dcigarette%20use%20among%20U.S.,%2C%2043.6%25%20reported%20current%20use.

28. Shalini Ramachandran, Betsy McKay, and Tom McGinty, "Millions of Kids Are on ADHA. For Many, It's the Start of a Drug Cascade," *Wall Street Journal*, updated November 19, 2025, accessed February 9, 2026, https://www.wsj.com/health/wellness/kids-adhd-drugs-medication-06dfa0b7?st=ubinPL&reflink=article_email_share.
29. *Constant Companion: A Week in the Life of a Young Person's Smartphone Use* (Common Sense, 2023), https://www.commonsensemedia.org/sites/default/files/research/report/2023-cs-smartphone-research-report_final-for-web.pdf.
30. "The New Normal: Parents, Teens, and Devices Around the World," Common Sense Media, October 1, 2019, https://www.commonsensemedia.org/research/the-new-normal-parents-teens-and-devices-around-the-world.
31. Mark Sellman, "Students 'Will Spend 25 Years on Their Mobiles,'" *Times,* June 22, 2025, https://www.thetimes.com/uk/technology-uk/article/average-young-person-25-years-phone-screen-time-hwt76mnpq#:~:text=The%20.
32. "Monitoring the Future Dataset: Satisfied with Life (12th Grade)," https://docs.google.com/spreadsheets/d/1OIDICfXkeBR_xXMvsGNUTbFaSPYTX20hw8xMrhIOpVo/edit?gid=437145853#gid=437145853.
33. For example, Edward L. Deci with Richard Flaste, *Why We Do What We Do: Understanding Self-Motivation* (Penguin, 1996); Viktor E. Frankl with Harold S. Kushner and William J. Winslade, *Man's Search for Meaning* (Beacon Press, 2006); Victor J. Stretcher, *Life on Purpose: How Living for What Matters Most Changes Everything* (HarperOne, 2016).
34. Carol S. Dweck, *Mindset: The New Psychology of Success* (Random House, 2006).
35. Daniel T. Willingham, *Why Don't Students like School?: A Cognitive*

Scientist Answers Questions About How the Mind Works and What It Means for the Classroom (Jossey-Bass, 2009), 127.

36. Ibid.
37. I got this example from my pastor, Jonathan Pokluda, who is even bigger than I am, so it is an even more ridiculous aspiration for him. In the end, neither of us will be jockeys.
38. Meg Jay, *The Defining Decade: Why* Your Twenties Matter—and How to Make the Most of Them Now (Twelve, 2021).
39. Emma Goldberg, "Is Today's Self-Help Teaching Everyone to Be a Jerk?" *New York Times*, updated August 25, 2025, accessed February 9, 2026, https://www.nytimes.com/2025/08/25/style/self-help-books-columns-readers.html.
40. To be fair, Jefferson's version of happiness was based on Aristotle's Greek term *eudaimonia*—the pursuit of virtue that results in well-being and flourishing—which is much more like the definition of *joy* I am using than our modern conception of happiness.
41. Molly Young, "My Miserable Week in the 'Happiest Country on Earth,'" *New York Times Magazine*, updated May 2, 2025, accessed February 9, 2026, https://www.nytimes.com/2025/05/02/magazine/finland-happiest-country.html?campaign_id=190&emc=edit_ufn_20250513&instance_id=154413&nl=from-the-times&regi_id=65920593&segment_id=197848&user_id=2723a4682d073ec079eb77ea1fdf8224.
42. The quiz is based on the work of David Almeida and Susan Charles. It can be found at https://www.nytimes.com/interactive/2025/04/30/magazine/what-makes-me-happy-quiz.html?campaign_id=190&emc=edit_ufn_20250505&instance_id=153886&nl=from-the-times&regi_id=65920593&segment_id=197324&user_id=2723a4682d073ec079eb77ea1fdf8224.
43. Martin E. P. Seligman, *Authentic Happiness: Using the New Positive Psychology to Realize Your Potential for Lasting Fulfillment* (Free Press, 2002).
44. Jonathan Haidt, *The Happiness Hypothesis: Finding Modern Truth in Ancient Wisdom* (Basic Books, 2005).
45. Gretchen Rubin, *The Happiness Project: Or, Why I Spent a Year Trying*

to Sing in the Morning, Clean My Closets, Fight Right, Read Aristotle, and Generallly Have More Fun (Harper, 2009).

46. Arthur C. Brooks, *The Happiness Files: Insights on Work and Life* (Harvard Business Review, 2025).
47. Cammack et al., "*Vital Signs.*"
48. Ellen Langer with Alison Beard, "Mindfulness in the Age of Complexity," *Harvard Business Review*, 2014, https://hbr.org/2014/03/mindfulness-in-the-age-of-complexity.
49. For example, in 1979, Jon Kabat-Zinn founded a program known as Mindfulness-Based Stress Reduction. There is significant evidence that this program of classes and daily meditation has improved physical, mental, emotional, and psychological conditions.

CHAPTER 2

1. Jellie Sierksma and Kristin Shutts, "The Unintended Negative Consequences of Help in Childhood," *Current Directions in Psychological Science* 34, no. 4 (2025): 247–52, https://doi.org/10.1177/09637214251323594.
2. Hu, N., Chen, K., Ye, L., Liu, H., Cai, D., Zhang, H., et al., "Associations Between Overparenting and Offspring's Mental Health: A Meta-analysis of Multiple Moderators," *Behavioral Sciences* 15, no 9: 1235. https://doi.org/10.3390/bs15091235.
3. High school students (4.2 percent) in wealthier areas are more likely than students (1.6 percent) in poorer areas to have a 504 plan that allows them additional time on tests. Three examples: At Scarsdale High School in New York, "one in five students is eligible for extra time or another accommodation such as a separate room for taking the SAT or ACT. At Weston High School in Connecticut, it is one in four. At Newton North High School outside Boston, it's one in three." Douglas Belkin, Jennifer Levitz, and Melissa Korn, "Many More Students, Especially the Affluent, Get Extra Time to Take the SAT," *Wall Street Journal*, updated May 2019, accessed February 9, 2026, https://www.wsj.com/articles/many-more-students-especially-the-affluent-get-extra-time-to-take-the-sat-11558450347?mod=e2tw&mod=article_inline.

4. The Learning Disabilities Association of America slammed people who abuse the system in a statement found at http://nypost.com/2024/03/27/us-news/private-school-students-get-fake-adhd-diagnoses-boost-sat/. "These actions hurt all individuals with disabilities, including those with learning disabilities, by perpetuating the misconceptions that many students who obtain accommodations on college admissions do not have disabilities."
5. Russell Shaw, "When Helicopter Parents Touch Down—at College," Atlantic, updated November 2, 2025, accessed February 10, 2026, https://www.theatlantic.com/family/2025/11/trailing-helicopter-parent-kids-college/684768/.
6. "University of California San Diego," *U.S. News & World* Report, updated 2016, accessed February 10, 2026, https://www.usnews.com/best-colleges/university-of-california-san-diego-1317.
7. Senate–Administration Working Group on Admissions, "Senate–Administration Workgroup on Admissions: Final Report," updated November 6, 2025, accessed February 10, 2026, https://senate.ucsd.edu/media/740347/sawg-report-on-admissions-review-docs.pdf.
8. Katherine E. Phillips, Kristina Conroy, Elizabeth L. Pinney, Jonathan S. Comer, and Philip C. Kendall, "School-Based Supports and Accommodations among Anxious Youth in Treatment," *Journal of Anxiety Disorders* 90 (August 2022): 102603, https://doi.org/10.1016/j.janxdis.2022.102603.
9. Ben Lovett and Alex Jordan, "Schools Are Accommodating Student Anxiety—and Making It Worse," updated October 16, 2025, accessed February 10, 2026, https://www.tc.columbia.edu/articles/2025/october/schools-are-accommodating-student-anxiety--and-making-it-worse/.
10. Morgan Housel, *Same As Ever: A Guide to What Never Changes* (Portfolio, 2023).
11. "The 2022 American Home Size Index," American Home Shield, updated May 2022, accessed February 10, 2026, https://www.ahs.com/home-matters/real-estate/the-2022-american-home-size-index/#:~:text=Over%20the%20last%2075%20years%2C%20the%20U.S.,15.7%25%20in%201950%20to%205.7%25%20in%202000.

12. Gloria Guzman and Melissa Kollar, "Income in the United States: 2023," United States Census Bureau, updated September 10, 2024, accessed February 10, 2026, https://www.census.gov/library/publications/2024/demo/p60-282.html#:~:text=Highlights,median%20household%20income%20since%202019.
13. Anikka Martin, "Food Prices and Spending," Economic Research Service, U.S. Department of Agriculture, updated September 29, 2025, accessed February 20, 2026, https://www.ers.usda.gov/data-products/ag-and-food-statistics-charting-the-essentials/food-prices-and-spending#:~:text=In%202024%2C%20U.S.%20consumers%20spent,at%205.6%20percent%20in%202024.
14. Housel, *Same as Ever*. Housel makes clear that these are average and not true for everyone in the United States. While I have updated some of the data, I would stipulate that I am speaking in broad, general terms about perceptions of material possessions contributing to happiness.
15. Max Kutner, "Two Tragic Years at L.A.'s Most Elite Private School," *Hollywood Reporter*, updated December 16, 2024, accessed February 10, 2026, https://www.hollywoodreporter.com/business/business-news/harvard-westlake-tragedies-students-1236085320/.
16. John Kay, *Obliquity: Why* Our Goals are Best Achieved Indirectly (Penguin, 2011), 16.
17. Greg Lukianoff and Jonathan Haidt, *The Coddling of the American Mind: How Good Intentions and Bad Ideas Are Setting Up a Generation for Failure* (Penguin, 2018); Haidt, *The Anxious Generation*.
18. Yeager, *10 to 25*, 72.
19. Dan Willingham, *Why Don't Students Like School* (Jossey-Bass, 2009), 3.
20. Jim VandeHei, Mike Allen, and Roy Schwartz, *Smart Brevity: The Power of Saying More with Less* (Workman, 2022).
21. Lukianoff and Haidt, *The Coddling of the American Mind*.
22. Janine Willis and Alexander Todorov, "First Impressions: Making Up Your Mind After a 100-Ms Exposure to a Face," *Association for Psychological Science, Princeton University* 17, no. 7 (2006): 592–98, https://web.archive.org/web/20140715094146/http://psych.princeton.edu/psychology/research/todorov/pdf/Willis%26Todorov-PsychScience.pdf.

23. I am a professor of educational leadership and a parent. I am not a psychologist, psychiatrist, or medical doctor, so I certainly do not want to contribute to this problem.
24. Abigail Shrier, *Bad Therapy: Why the Kids Aren't Growing Up* (Sentinel, 2024).
25. Kao-Ping Chua, Anna Volerman, Jason Zhang, Joanna Hua, and Rena M. Conti, "Antidepressant Dispensing to US Adolescents and Young Adults: 2016–2022," *Pediatrics* 153, no. 3, https://doi.org/10.1542/peds.2023-064245; https://publications.aap.org/pediatrics/article/153/3/e2023064245/196655/Antidepressant-Dispensing-to-US-Adolescents-and?autologincheck=redirected.
26. Ibid.
27. "Children's Mental Health Data," U.S. Centers for Disease Control, updated June 5, 2025, accessed February 10, 2026, https://www.cdc.gov/children-mental-health/data-research/index.html#:~:text=More%20than%20half%20(55%25),unmet%20mental%20health%20care%20needs.
28. Olivia Sappenfield, Cinthya Alberto, Jessica Minnaert, Julie Donney, Lydie Lebrun-Harris, and Reem Ghandour, "Adolescent Mental and Behavioral Health, 2023," National Center for Biotechnology Information, National Library of Medicine, updated October 2024, accessed February 10, 2026, https://www.ncbi.nlm.nih.gov/books/NBK608531/.
29. Betsy McKay, Shalini Ramachandran, and John West, "'Girl, Take Your Crazy Pills!': Antidepressants Recast as a Hot Lifestyle Accessory," *Wall Street Journal*, updated October 18, 2025, accessed February 10, 2026, https://www.wsj.com/health/wellness/anti-depressants-lifestyle-accessory-3b66027d?st=K47R98&reflink=article_email_share.
30. Robb and Mann, "Boys in the Digital Wild."
31. "To Like or Dislike? Women's Complex Relationship with Social Media Influencers," *Reboot: Elevating Critical Thinking*, updated November 29, 2023, accessed February 10, 2026, https://reboot-foundation.org/research/to-like-or-dislike-womens-complex-relationship-with-social-media-influencers/.

32. Jon Ebert, a clinical psychologist and associate professor of clinical psychiatry and behavioral sciences at Vanderbilt University Medical Center, believes that healthy doses of adversity and supportive relationships are key. He says, "Therapists should be helpful guides for kids, but not the heroes in the development story. Empowering families, caregivers and mentors to walk alongside children and youth are key to helping kids grow through adversity." Therapists can certainly provide coping tools and supports, but families [caregiving systems] are key to helping kids grow stronger when life's winds start blowing. Good therapists empower those important families/caregivers.
33. Robert Waldinger and Marc Schulz, *The Good Life: Lessons from the World's Longest Scientific Study of Happiness* (Simon & Schuster, 2023), 3. While the study began with only men and Harvard and was therefore somewhat limited in its generalizable findings, others, including women and more socioeconomically diverse participants, have been added.

CHAPTER 3

1. This is a pseudonym.
2. This is a pseudonym.
3. We won't explore the forty-billion-dollar youth sports complex that preys on parents' aspirations for high-school and college athletic glory for their kids. For many athletes and parents, this has become a source of destructive struggle that does not lead to happiness or joy. "Youth Sports Facts: Challenges," Project Play, Aspen Institute, accessed February 10, 2026, https://projectplay.org/youth-sports/facts/challenges#:~:text=The%20Aspen%20Institute%20estimated%20U.S.,philanthropy%20and%20the%20private%20sector.
4. Meg Jay, *The Defining Decade*; Meg Jay, *The Twentysomething Treatment: A Revolutionary Remedy for an Uncertain Age* (Simon & Schuster, 2024).
5. Valentin Emslander et al., "Teacher–Student Relationships and Student Outcomes: A Systematic Second-Order Meta-Analytic Review," *Psychological Bulletin* 151, no. 3 (2025): 365–97, https://doi.org/10.1037/bul0000461.

6. John Steinbeck, "Like Captured Fireflies," accessed February 10, 2026, https://www.alisonpask.de/wp-content/uploads/2012/08/john-steinbeck-like-captured-fireflies.pdf.

CHAPTER 4

1. Waldinger and Schulz, *The Good Life*, 29.
2. "Americans Haven't Found a Satisfying Alternative to God," *New York Times*, updated April 18, 2025, accessed February 10, 2026, https://www.nytimes.com/2025/04/18/style/religion-america.html. Full disclosure: As a Christian, I believe that the only immortal things we interact with each day are the human beings God puts in our paths. What we do with our relationships matters for eternity, because we have hope, we serve a relational God, and we are the overflow of that relationship. Throughout this book, I will try to appeal to the common grace of Truth to appeal to as many readers as possible. However, there may be points where someone who does not start with the belief that we are created beings, made in the image of our Creator, might reject some of my foundational premises. I am praying that curiosity and our shared humanity will allow minds to be open to see the hope in the belief that we have an eternal purpose and are more loved than we could ever imagine.
3. Waldinger and Schulz, *The Good Life*.
4. Aristotle, *Nicomachean Ethics*, 2nd ed., trans. T. Irwin (Hackett, 1999).
5. Gal. 5:14 (English Standard Version).
6. Thomas Aquinas, *Summa Theologica: Complete English Translation in Five Volumes* (Ave Maria, 1948).
7. Tyler J. VanderWeele and Matthew T. Lee, "Love and Human Flourishing," *International Journal of Well-Being* 15, no. 4 (2025): 1–31, https://doi.org/10.5502/ijw.v15i4.4663.
8. Timothy Keller, *The Reason for God: Belief in an Age of Skepticism* (Viking, 2008), 170.
9. Tyler J. VanderWeele, Byron R. Johnson, Piotr T. Bialowolski et al., "The Global Flourishing Study: Study Profile and Initial Results on Flourishing," *Nature Mental Health* 637, updated April 30, 2025, accessed February 10, 2026, https://doi.org/10.1038/s44220-025-00423-5.

10. Ibid.
11. Daniel Coyle, *Flourish: The Art of Building Meaning, Joy, and Fulfillment* (Bantam, 2026).
12. David Brooks, "Why More People in the World Are Feeling Hopeful (Except Us)," *New York Times*, updated August 7, 2025, accessed February 10, 2026, https://www.nytimes.com/2025/08/07/opinion/happiness-community-wealth.html?smid=nytcore-ios-share&referringSource=articleShare.
13. This is a pseudonym.
14. Sheryl Sandberg and Adam Grant, *Option B: Facing Adversity, Building Resistance, and Finding Joy* (Knopf, 2017).
15. John Stuart Mill, *Autobiography* (Penguin Classics, 1873, 1990), chapter 5.
16. Daniel Gilbert, *Stumbling on Happiness* (Knopf, 2006); John Kay, *Obliquity*.
17. Aekyoung Kim and Sam J. Maglio, "Happiness Depletes Me: Seeking Happiness Impairs Limited Resources and Self-Regulation," *Applied Psychology: Health and Well-Being*, 17, no. 1 (2025), updated January 30, 2025, accessed February 10, 2026, https://doi.org/10.1111/aphw.70000; F. K. Zerwas, B. Q. Ford, O. P. John, and I. B. Mauss, "Unpacking Pursuit of Happiness: Being Concerned About Happiness but not Aspiring to Happiness Is Linked with Negative Meta-Emotions and Worse Well-Being," *Emotion* 24, no. 8 (2024): 1789–802, https://doi.org/10.1037/emo0001381.
18. Putnam with Romney Garrett, *The Upswing*.
19. Tom Huddleston Jr., "Success Requires 'Ample Does of Pain,' Billionare Nvidia CEO Tells Stanford Students: 'I Hope Suffering Happens to You,'" CNBC.com, updated March 15, 2024, accessed February 10, 2026, https://www.cnbc.com/2024/03/15/nvidia-ceo-huang-at-stanford-pain-and-suffering-breeds-success.html.

CHAPTER 5

1. Nataliya Kosmyna, Eugene Hauptmann, Ye Tong Yuan, Jessica Situ, Xian-Hao Liao, Ashly Vivian Beresnitzky, et al., "Your Brain on ChatGPT: Accumulation of Cognitive Debt When Using an

AI Assistant for Essay Writing Task," Cornell University, updated December 31, 2025, accessed February 10, 2026, https://doi.org/10.48550/ARXIV.2506.08872.

2. "2025 Edelman Trust Barometer: Global Report: Trust and the Crisis of Grievance," Edelman Trust Institute, accessed February 10, 2026, https://www.edelman.com/sites/g/files/aatuss191/files/2025-01/2025%20Edelman%20Trust%20Barometer%20Global%20Report_01.23.25.pdf.
3. Esteban Ortiz-Ospina, "Expectancy: What Does This Actually Mean?" Our World in Data, updated August 18, 2017, accessed February 10, 2026, https://ourworldindata.org/life-expectancy-how-is-it-calculated-and-how-should-it-be-interpreted.
4. Saloni Dattani, Fiona Spooner, Hannah Ritchie, and Max Roser, "Child and Infant Mortality," Our World in Data, updated 2024, accessed February 10, 2026, https://ourworldindata.org/child-mortality.
5. Max Roser, "Extreme Poverty: How Far Have We Come, and How Far Do We Still Have to Go?" Our World in Data, updated August 27, 2023, accessed February 10, 2026, https://ourworldindata.org/extreme-poverty-in-brief.
6. Benedict Vigers, "More People Globally Living Better Lives," Gallup, updated July 29, 2025, accessed February 10, 2026, https://news.gallup.com/poll/692816/people-globally-living-better-lives.aspx#:~:text=Gallup's%20Life%20Evaluation%20Index%2C%20based,Everyone%20else%20is%20%22struggling.%22.
7. Ibid.
8. S. F. Maier and M. E. P. Seligman, "Learned Helplessness at Fifty: Insights from Neuroscience," *Psychological Review* 123, no. 4 (2025): 349–67, https://doi.org/10.1037/rev0000033.
9. "Historical Living Arrangements of Adults," United States Census Bureau, updated December 2026, accessed February 10, 2026, https://www.census.gov/data/tables/time-series/demo/families/adults.html.
10. Angela Duckworth, *Grit: The Power of Passion and Perseverance* (Scribner, 2016).
11. Tyler J. VanderWeele, "Hope and Rational Optimism," *Psychology Today*, updated November 1, 2024, accessed February 10, 2026,

https://www.psychologytoday.com/us/blog/human-flourishing/202410/hope-and-rational-optimism.

12. Meg Jay, *The Defining Decade*.
13. Cal Newport, *So Good They Can't Ignore You: Why Skills Trump Passion in the Quest for Work You Love* (Grand Central, 2012).
14. Angela Duckworth and Mike Maughan, hosts, *No Stupid Questions*, podcast, episode 221, "Why Are We So Pessimistic?" n.d., https://podcasts.apple.com/us/podcast/no-stupid-questions/id1510056899?i=1000677961954.
15. Daniel Duke, "How Do You Turn Around a Low-Performing School?" (ASCD Annual Conference, New Orleans, LA, 2008).
16. A world-renowned education expert challenged me about this turtle and crab metaphor. He wrote in the margins of an early draft of this book, "Anthropomorphism at its best. Sea turtles do all this to protect themselves from predators. They do not strive for happiness but for survival. I want more than that!" I agree on two counts: 1) Only humans can experience true joy, and 2) sometimes all we are capable of is surviving. In reality, we want to be more than turtles. For us to move beyond sea turtle survival, joy must be found in a life lived for and with others. We need more than aspiration. We cannot just hope that some kids, or even all kids, will thrive. We must ensure each kid is engaged and receiving feedback that leads to flourishing in the form of joy. Doing that will require hard work and gritty optimism, but I see examples of that in stories like Ms. Parks' and New Hope's story and that make me want to be a turtle and not a crab! How do we find more of those stories?

CHAPTER 6

1. "6 September (1955): Flannery O'Connor to Betty Hester," This Day in Lettres, *American Reader*, accessed February 10, 2026, https://theamericanreader.com/6-september-1955-flannery-oconnor/.
2. Emily Tomasik and Katerina Eva Matsa, "1 in 5 Americans Now Regularly Get News on TikTok, up Sharply from 2020," Pew Research Center, updated September 25, 2025, accessed February 10, 2026, https://www.pewresearch.org/short-reads/2025/09/25/1-in-5-americans-now-regularly-get news-on-tiktok-up-sharply-from-2020

/#:~:text=A%20fifth%20of%20U.S.%20adults,How%20we%20did%20this.

3. Lan Nguyen, Jared Walters, Siddharth Paul, Shay Monreal Ijurco, Georgia E. Rainey, Nupur Parekh, et al., "Feeds, Feelings, and Focus: A Systematic Review and Meta-Analysis Examining the Cognitive and Mental Health Correlates of Short-Form Video Use," *Psychological Bulletin* 151, no. 9 (2025): 1125–46, https://doi.org/10.1037/bul0000498.
4. Nicholas Light, Philip M. Fernbach, Nathaniel Rabb, Mugur V. Geana, and Steven A. Sloman, "Knowledge Overconfidence Is Associated with Anti-Consensus Views on Controversial Scientific Issues," *Science Advances* 8, no. 29 (2022), https://doi.org/10.1126/sciadv.abo0038.
5. In the epilogue of his essay, Tolkien asserts that fantasy stories evoke joy when they point us to deeper Truth. J. R. R. Tolkien, *Tolkien on Fairy-Stories*, eds. Verlyn Flieger and Douglas A. Anderson (HarperCollins, 2014).
6. Ibid.
7. Arthur C. Brooks, *The Happiness Files*, 13.
8. Grant Wiggins and Jay McTighe, *Understanding by Design*, 2nd ed. (Association for Supervision & Curriculum Development, 2005).
9. Ibid.
10. Dan Heath, *Reset: How to Change What's Not Working* (Avid Reader, 2025).
11. Grant Wiggins and Jay McTighe, *Understanding by Design.* Riess and Kraft-Todd offer a useful tool for enhancing empathy through nonverbal communication: Helen Riess and Gordon Kraft-Todd, "E.M.P.A.T.H.Y.: A Tool to Enhance Nonverbal Communication Between Clinicians and Their Patients," *Academic Medicine* 89, no. 8 (2014), 1108–12, https://doi.org/10.1097/ACM.0000000000000287.
12. John Henry Newman, *The Idea of a University* (Yale University Press, 1996).
13. Greg Lukianoff and Jonathan Haidt, *The Coddling of the American Mind.* Lukianoff and Haidt do a masterful job making this point in far more detail and more articulately than I could.

14. Brian Lowery, *Selfless: The Social Creation of "You"* (Harper, 2023), 5, 15.
15. Ibram X. Kendi, *How to Be an Antiracist* (One World, 2019).
16. Rachel Crowley, "Genetics by the Numbers," *Biomedical Beat Blog*, National Institute of General Medical Sciences, updated April 24, 2024, accessed February 10, 2026, https://nigms.nih.gov/biobeat/2024/04/genetics-by-the-numbers.

CHAPTER 7

1. Robert D. Putnam with Shaylyn Romney Garrett, *The Upswing*.
2. Jonathan Rothwell, "Teens Spend Average of 4.8 Hours on Social Media Per Day," Gallup, updated October 13, 2023, accessed February 10, 2026, https://news.gallup.com/poll/512576/teens-spend-average-hours-social-media-per-day.aspx.
3. Michael B. Robb and Supreet Mann, "Talk, Trust, and Trade-Offs: How and Why Teens Use AI Companions," Common Sense Media, updated 2025, accessed February 10, 2026, https://www.commonsensemedia.org/sites/default/files/research/report/talk-trust-and-trade-offs_2025_web.pdf.
4. Ibid.
5. Bethanie Maples, Merve Cerit, Aditya Vishwanath, and Roy Pea, "Loneliness and Suicide Mitigation for Students Using GPT3-Enabled Chatbots," *Npj Mental Health Research* 3, no. 1 (2024): 4, https://doi.org/10.1038/s44184-023-00047-6.
6. Ivo Petrov, Jasper Dekoninck, and Martin Vechev, "BrokenMath: A Benchmark for Sycophancy in Theorem Proving with LLMs," *arXiv*, updated October 6, 2025, accessed February 10, 2026, https://arxiv.org/pdf/2510.04721.
7. Michael B. Robb and Supreet Mann, "Talk, Trust, and Trade-Offs."
8. Robert D. Putnam with Shaylyn Romney Garrett, *The Upswing*, 6–7.
9. Robert D. Putnam, *Bowling Alone: The Collapse and Revival of American Community* (Simon & Schuster, 2000).
10. Nicholas Light, Philip M. Fernbach, Nathaniel Rabb, Mugur V. Geana, and Steven A. Sloman, "Knowledge Overconfidence."

11. Adam Grant, *Think Again: The Power of Knowing What You Don't Know* (Viking, 2021).
12. This is a pseudonym.
13. Unlike computers, which are bound by the limits of analyzing data and looking for patterns, as humans we can move beyond probability to what might be possible. Stories help us understand what might be possible. Angus Fletcher, who leads Project Narrative at Ohio State University, has written about this extensively. Angus Fletcher, *Primal Intelligence: You Are Smarter Than You Know* (Penguin, 2025).
14. Yeager describes a college professor who builds on David Merton's concept of "anticipatory socialization," where we help prepare kids for a "world that they do not yet belong to." We do this by normalizing struggle and emphasizing purpose. Yeager, *10 to 25*, 371.

CHAPTER 8

1. Ayjay, "Teachers at the Margins," *The Homebound Symphony*, October 23, 2019, https://blog.ayjay.org/teachers-at-the-margins/.
2. Angus Fletcher, *Primal Intelligence*.
3. I asked Grace's permission to share this story. I am so grateful to her for allowing others to learn from her vulnerability and my lowest point as a parent. She knows, and you all should know, she is in no way a disappointment to her family. She is truly one of the greatest gifts we have ever received. I love you more than you will know on this side of eternity, Grace.
4. Christopher Emdin, *For White Folks Who Teach in the Hood . . . and the Rest of Y'all Too: Reality Pedagogy and Urban Education* (Beacon, 2016); Matthew Dicks, *Storyworthy: Engage, Teach, Persuade, and Change Your Life Through the Power of Storytelling* (New World Library, 2018).
5. Brené Brown, *Daring Greatly: How the Courage to Be Vulnerable Transforms the Way We Live, Love, Parent, and Lead* (Avery, 2012).
6. While not in this book, David Brooks shared these three questions from the stage as he was presenting. David Brooks, *How to Know a Person: The Art of Seeing Others Deeply and Being Deeply Seen* (Random House, 2023).

7. Matthew Dicks, *Storyworthy*.
8. David Brooks, *How to Know a Person*; Amanda Ripley, *High Conflict: Why We Get Trapped and How We Get Out* (Simon & Schuster, 2021).
9. Will Storr, *The Science of Storytelling: Why Stories Make Us Human and How to Tell Them Better* (Abrams, 2020); Will Storr, *A Story Is a Deal: How* to Use the Science of Storytelling to Lead, Motivate, and Persuade (Piatkus, 2025); Matthew Dicks, *Storyworthy*; Matthew Dicks, *Stories Sell: Storyworthy Strategies to Grow Your Business and Brand* (New World Library, 2024); Karen Eber, *The Perfect Story: How to Tell Stories That Inform, Influence, and Inspire* (Harper Horizon, 2023).
10. Matthew Dicks, *Storyworthy*; Matthew Dicks, *Stories Sell*.
11. Karen Eber, *The Perfect Story*.

CHAPTER 9

1. These quotations all came from feedback on the original book-product description.
2. How we transcend suffering diverges, but this realization that life and suffering are inextricably linked is common to the human experience and an example of common grace.
3. Adam Grant, host, *Worklife with Adam Grant*, podcast, "ReThinking: What We're Getting Wrong About Mental Health with RaQuel Hopkins," October 6, 2025, https://shows.acast.com/worklife-with-adam-grant/episodes/raquel-hopkins.
4. Laura Landro, "Patients Are Diagnosing Themselves With Home Tests, Devices and Chatbots," *Wall Street Journal*, updated September 30, 2025, accessed February 10, 2026, https://www.wsj.com/health/healthcare/patient-self-medical-treatment-tools-85b43eaa?campaign_id=9&emc=edit_nn_20251001&instance_id=163590&mod=hp_featst_pos5&nl=the-morning&regi_id=65920593&segment_id=206943&user_id=2723a4682d073ec079eb77ea1fdf8224; Ryan K. McBain, "Teens Are Using Chatbots as Therapists. That's Alarming," *New York Times*, updated August 25, 2025, accessed February 10, 2026, https://www.nytimes.com/2025/08/25/opinion/teen-mental-health-chatbots.html.

5. Joseph Bernstein, "It Makes Sense That People See A.I. as God," *New York Times*, updated January 23, 2026, accessed February 10, 2026, https://www.nytimes.com/2026/01/23/style/ai-algorithm-god-religion.html?smid=nytcore-ios-share.
6. Ryan K. McBain, "Teens Are Using Chatbots."
7. Angus Fletcher, *Primal Intelligence*.
8. Jennifer Breheny Wallace, *Never Enough: When Achievement Culture Becomes Toxic—and What We Can Do About It* (Portfolio, 2023).
9. Brené Brown, *Daring Greatly*.
10. This is a pseudonym.
11. Victoria M. E. Bridgland, Payton J. Jones, and Benjamin W. Bellet, "A Meta-Analysis of the Efficacy of Trigger Warnings, Content Warnings, and Content Notes," *Clinical Psychological Science* 12, no. 4:751–71, https://doi.org/10.1177/21677026231186625.

CHAPTER 10

1. Supreet Mann, Angela Calvin, Amanda Lenhart, and Michael B. Robb, "The Common Sense Census: Media Use by Kids Zero to Eight, 2025," Common Sense Media, updated 2025, accessed February 10, 2026, https://www.commonsensemedia.org/sites/default/files/research/report/2025-common-sense-census-web-2.pdf.
2. We adapted twenty-nine questions in class from two books and a groundbreaking 1997 paper. We were not aiming for the thirty-six questions that lead to love, so we adapted them to deepen engagement. Ran Barzilay, Samuel D. Pimentel, Kate T. Tran, Elina Visoki, David Pagliaccio, and Randy P. Auerbach, "Smartphone Ownership, Age of Smartphone Acquisition, and Health Outcomes in Early Adolescence," *Pediatrics*, updated December 1, 2025, accessed February 10, 2026, https://doi.org/10.1542/peds.2025-072941.
3. Annelise Reinwald, "Twenty-two States Enacted K–12 Cellphone Bans So Far in 2025," Ballotpedia, updated August 8, 2025, accessed February 10, 2026, https://news.ballotpedia.org/2025/08/08/twenty-two-states-enacted-k-12-cellphone-bans-so-far-in-2025/.
4. Ran Barzilay, Samuel D. Pimentel, Kate T. Tran, Elina Visoki, David Pagliaccio, and Randy P. Auerbach, "Smartphone Ownership."

5. David N. Figlio and Umet Ozek, "The Impact of Cellphone Bans in Schools on Student Outcomes: Evidence from Florida," Working Paper No. 34388 (National Bureau of Economic Research, October 2025), https://drive.google.com/file/d/18zZ4GeQE49HFkkVPwOu1lYNlaDtE29N5/view.
6. Jean Twenge, "The Screen That Ate Your Child's Education," *New York Times*, updated November 16, 2025, accessed February 10, 2025, https://www.nytimes.com/2025/11/16/opinion/laptop-classroom-test-scores.html.
7. Michael B. Robb and Supreet Mann, "Teens and Pornography," Common Sense Media, updated 2023, accessed February 10, 2026, https://www.commonsensemedia.org/sites/default/files/research/report/2022-teens-and-pornography-final-web.pdf.
8. Susan M. Ravizza, Mitchell G. Uitvlugt, and Kimberly M. Fenn, "Logged In and Zoned Out: How Laptop Internet Use Relates to Classroom Learning," *Psychological Science* 28, no. 2 (2017): 171–80, https://doi.org/10.1177/0956797616677314.
9. Pablo Delgado, Cristina Vargas, Rakefet Ackerman, and Ladislao Salmerón, "Don't Throw Away Your Printed Books: A Meta-Analysis on the Effects of Reading Media on Reading Comprehension," *Educational Research Review* 25 (November 2018): 23–38, https://doi.org/10.1016/j.edurev.2018.09.003.
10. Ladislao Salmerón, Cristina Vargas, Pablo Delgado, and Naomi Baron, "Relation Between Digital Tool Practices in the Language Arts Classroom and Reading Comprehension Scores," *Reading and Writing* 36, no. 1 (2023): 175–94, https://doi.org/10.1007/s11145-022-10295-1.
11. Abraham E. Flanigan, Jordan Wheeler, Tiphaine Colliot, Junrong Lu, and Kenneth A. Kiewra, "Typed versus Handwritten Lecture Notes and College Student Achievement: A Meta-Analysis," *Educational Psychology Review* 36, no. 3 (2024): 78, https://doi.org/10.1007/s10648-024-09914-w.
12. Gorka Ibaibarriaga, Joana Acha, and Manuel Perea, "The Impact of Handwriting and Typing Practice in Children's Letter and Word Learning: Implications for Literary Development," *Journal of*

Experimental Child Psychology 253 (May 2025): 106195, https://doi.org/10.1016/j.jecp.2025.106195.

13. Zach Hrynowski, "Gen Z Students More Engaged in School, Ready for the Future," Gallup, updated August 26, 2025, accessed February 10, 2026, https://news.gallup.com/poll/694238/gen-students-engaged-school-ready-future.aspx#:~:text=In%202025%2C%20all%20eight%20measures,(78%25%20versus%2070%25.
14. C. S. Lewis, *The Weight of Glory* (HarperCollins, 2001).
15. As a Christian, the belief that we serve a relational God who exists as a Trinity and has created us out of that overflow very much informs my view here. If we are immortal, as Lewis asserts, and we are made for relationship, then I believe we get glimpses of God and eternity through the relationships we experience with others as embodied souls. Obviously, a secular humanist or others from faith backgrounds different from my own could disagree, but my anchored belief in God makes me far more likely to deeply engage others rather than seek fleeting comfort.
16. Jonathan Haidt, *The Anxious Generation*.
17. Richard Louv, *Last Child in the Woods: Saving Our Children from Nature-Deficit Disorder*, updated and expanded edition (Algonquin, 2008).
18. Arthur Brooks, "You Need to Be Bored. Here's Why," posted August 26, 2025, by Harvard Business Review, YouTube, 5 min., 49 sec., https://www.youtube.com/watch?v=orQKfIXMiA8.
19. Ibid.
20. Amy Berry, *Reimagining Student Engagement: From Disrupting to Driving* (Corwin, 2022).

CHAPTER 11

1. Amy C. Edmondson, *The Fearless Organization: Creating Psychological Safety in the Workplace for Learning, Innovation, and Growth* (Wiley, 2018).
2. Greg Lukianoff and Jonathan Haidt, *The Coddling of the American Mind*.
3. At the time of publication, the last death that occurred in Pamplona

while running with the bulls was in 2009. Additionally, we have to teach our kids to drive. In no way do we need to run alongside bulls!

4. David S. Yeager, *10 to 25*.
5. Ibid.
6. "School Recess Strategies," U.S. Centers for Disease Control, updated April 25, 2019, accessed February 10, 2026, https://www.cdc.gov/healthyschools/physicalactivity/pdf/2019_04_25_SchoolRecess_strategies_508tagged.pdf.
7. "Explore 2024 NAEP Results for Science at Grade 8 and Mathematics and Reading at Grade 12," National Assessment of Educational Progress, accessed February 10, 2026, http://nces.ed.gov/nationsreportcard/.
8. "Recess," U.S. Centers for Disease Control, updated July 1, 2024, accessed February 10, 2026, https://www.cdc.gov/physical-activity-education/recess/index.html.
9. Deborah J. Rhea, Kelsey Kirby, Dennis Cheek, Yan Zhang, and G. Kate Webb, "The Impact of Recess on Chronic Stress Levels in Elementary School Children," *Children* 12, no. 7 (2025): 865, https://doi.org/10.3390/children12070865.
10. Jonathan Haidt, *The Anxious Generation*.
11. Ibid., 90.
12. Peter Gray, David F. Lancy, and David F. Bjorklund, "Decline in Independent Activity as a Cause of Decline in Children's Mental Well-Being: Summary of the Evidence," *Journal of Pediatrics* 260 (September 2023): 113352, https://doi.org/10.1016/j.jpeds.2023.02.004.
13. David S. Yeager, *10 to 25*.
14. Rachel Minkin and Juliana Menasce Horowitz, "Parenting in America Today: Mental Health Concerns Top the List of Worries for Parents; Most Say Being a Parent is Harder Than They Expected," Pew Research Center, updated January 24, 2023, accessed February 10, 2026, https://www.pewresearch.org/social-trends/2023/01/24/parenting-in-america-today/.
15. Kiley Hurst, Dana Braga, Shannon Greenwood, Chris Baronavski, and Michael Keegan, "How Today's Parents Say Their Approach to Parenting Does—or Doesn't—Match Their Own Upbringing," Pew

Research Center, updated January 24, 2023, accessed February 10, 2026, https://www.pewresearch.org/social-trends/2023/01/24/how-todays-parents-say-their-approach-to-parenting-does-or-doesnt-match-their-own-upbringing/.

16. Sarah Ockwell-Smith, *The Gentle Parenting Book: How to* Raise Calmer, Happier Children from Birth to Seven (Piatkus, 2021).
17. Ellen Gamerman, "Goodbye Gentle Parenting, Hello 'F— Around and Find Out,'" *Wall Street Journal*, updated July 25, 2025, accessed February 10, 2026, https://www.wsj.com/lifestyle/fafo-gentle-parenting-625da658?gaa_at=eafs&gaa_n=ASWzDAjqFQ8g_drTMMC6GbfbLnrdEoU_uypi7TGErVDN2ww3aFgLLWOOri303swDSVY%3D&gaa_ts=68a31f17&gaa_sig=4E6xjBgDiCYPVRhwOZtZa2vhm2J3zyP_oGICv3rB7RTP9jiBcYNdPu4uU_bomXFbJ-S8x1Byo1mjfjnZfb2ryA%3D%3D.
18. Pamela J. Cooper and Cheri J. Simonds, *Communication for the Classroom Teacher*, 8th ed. (Pearson, 2006).
19. This is a pseudonym.

CHAPTER 12

1. Will Guidara, *Unreasonable Hospitality: The Remarkable Power of Giving People More Than They Expect* (Optimism, 2022), 4.
2. *Merriam-Webster* Dictionary, "hospitable," accessed February 10, 2026, https://www.merriam-webster.com/dictionary/hospitable.
3. Erik Carter writes and speaks about this beautifully, particularly as it relates to people with disabilities. Erik W. Carter, "Dimensions of Belonging for Individuals with Intellectual and Developmental Disabilities," in *Belonging and Resilience in Individuals with Developmental Disabilities: Emerging Issues in Family and Individual Resilience*, ed. J. L. Jones and K. L. Gallus (Springer, 2021).
4. Carol S. Dweck, "From Needs to Goals and Representations: Foundations for a Unified Theory of Motivation, Personality, and Development," *Psychological Review* 124, no. 6 (2017): 689–719, https://doi.org/10.1037/rev0000082; David S. Yeager, *10 to 25*.
5. "Food Security in the U.S.—Key Statistics & Graphics," Economic

Research Service, U.S. Department of Agriculture, updated January 8, 2025, accessed February 10, 2026, https://www.ers.usda.gov/topics/food-nutrition-assistance/food-security-in-the-us/key-statistics-graphics#insecure.

6. This is a pseudonym.
7. This is a pseudonym.
8. A field used for soccer, field hockey, rugby, and Australian football.
9. A carnival.
10. Australians are less hospitable about American coffee, which I heard referred to as "coffee juice" and "undrinkable."
11. "Budgie smugglers" are a very limited-coverage type of swimwear found primarily in Australia.
12. CNN, "Stephen Colbert and Anderson Cooper's beautiful conversation about grief," posted August 17, 2019, by Mostly Water, YouTube, 21 min., 13 sec., https://www.youtube.com/watch?v=YB46h1koicQ.

CHAPTER 13

1. David Brooks, *The Second Mountain: The Quest for a Moral Life* (Random House, 2019).
2. Ashley Humphrey, Rebecca Szoka, and Brock Bastian, "When the Pursuit of Happiness Backfires: The Role of Negative Emotion Valuation," *Journal of Positive Psychology* 17, no. 5 (2022): 611–19, https://doi.org/10.1080/17439760.2021.1897869; Arthur Brooks, *The Happiness Files.*
3. Matthew McConaughey writes and talks about this extensively. Even when he delivers an Academy Award–winning–level performance, there is still the dissatisfaction of it not matching what was in his mind. Matthew McConaughey, *Poems and Prayers* (Crown, 2025).
4. Elizabeth M. Bounds, Juliette L. Ratchford, and Sarah A. Schnitker, "Profile Membership of Self-Worth Contingencies Predicts Well-Being, Virtues, and Values," *Journal of Happiness Studies* 25, no. 4 (2024): 42, https://doi.org/10.1007/s10902-024-00758-3; Perry L. Glanzer, Jessica Martin, Elizabeth Bounds, Karen K. Melton,

Theodore F. Cockle, and Sarah A. Schnitker, "Sources of Self-Worth in U.S. College Students: A Grounded Typology," *Journal of College Student Development* 65, no. 5 (2024): 507–26, https://doi.org/10.1353/csd.2024.a940718.

5. Pablo S. Torre, "How (and Why) Athletes Go Broke," *Sports Illustrated*, March 23, 2009, https://tartaros.lu/uploads/cgblog/id18/19_1f0e3dad.pdf.
6. Cath Bishop, "Norway's All-Conquering Winter Olympians Have a Message for Us All—and It's Not What You Think," *The Guardian*, February 26, 2026, https://www.theguardian.com/sport/2026/feb/26/norway-winter-olympics-message-for-us-all.
7. Rainer Maria Rilke, *Letters to a Young Poet*, trans. M. D. Herter Norton (W. W. Norton, 1993), 27.
8. Robert Waldinger and Marc Schulz, *The Good Life*.

ABOUT THE AUTHOR

Spanning a three-decade career, Jon Eckert has taught at almost every level. He taught and coached middle-grade students outside of Chicago and Nashville for twelve years, gaining an up-close view of the tumultuous lives of students. Through his doctoral work at Vanderbilt University and his time at the U.S. Department of Education, he glimpsed the thirty-thousand-foot view that policymakers have of the lives of students and families. A desire to elevate the perspectives of educators and parents for leaders moved him into higher education at Wheaton College and Baylor University. Through his work as the Lynda and Robert Copple Professor of Educational Leadership at the Baylor Center for School Leadership, he has written numerous books and articles and learned from educators on four continents. He lives in Waco, Texas, with his wife, Carolyn, and they are the grateful parents of Ben, Sarah, and Grace.